BLINDING FLASH

The Courage and Sacrifice of a Bomb Disposal Hero,
Ken Revis MBE

BLINDING FLASH

THE COURAGE AND SACRIFICE OF A BOMB DISPOSAL HERO, KEN REVIS MBE

John Frayn Turner
Foreword by
Sir Brian Horrocks KCB, KBE, DSO, MC, LL.D

FRONTLINE
BOOKS

BLINDING FLASH
The Courage and Sacrifice of a Bomb Disposal Hero, Ken Revis MBE

First published in Great Britain in 1962 by George Harrap & Co. Ltd., London.
This edition published in in 2023 by Frontline Books,
an imprint of Pen & Sword Books Ltd., Yorkshire - Philadelphia

Copyright © John Frayn Turner, 2023

ISBN: 978-1-39904-596-4

Typeset in Chennai, India
by Lapiz Digital Services.

Printed and bound by CPI UK

Pen & Sword Books Ltd incorporates the imprints of Pen & Sword Archaeology,
Air World Books, Atlas, Aviation, Battleground, Discovery, Family History,
History, Maritime, Military, Naval, Politics, Social History, Transport, True Crime,
Claymore Press, Frontline Books, Praetorian Press, Seaforth Publishing and
White Owl

For a complete list of Pen & Sword titles please contact:

PEN & SWORD BOOKS LTD
47 Church Street, Barnsley, South Yorkshire, S70 2AS, UK.
E-mail: enquiries@pen-and-sword.co.uk
Website: www.pen-and-sword.co.uk

Or

PEN AND SWORD BOOKS,
1950 Lawrence Road, Havertown, PA 19083, USA
E-mail: Uspen-and-sword@casematepublishers.com
Website: www.penandswordbooks.com

CONTENTS

PUBLISHER'S NOTE

John Frayn Turner's moving biography of Ken Revis MBE was first published in 1962. Consequently, some of the terminology and descriptions used, such as a number of those referring to blind people or individuals with disabilities, might be considered dated by today's readers. However, in order to preserve John's work, we have endeavoured to keep any alterations or changes to the absolute minimum.

FOREWORD

By Sir Brian Horrocks KCB, KBE, DSO, MC, LL.D

Courage and determination are the two outstanding qualities that emerge from this remarkable story. First of all, that special brand of ice-cold courage required in the handling of enemy bombs; and, secondly, the personal courage and determination of two young people, Ken Revis and his wife, Jo, who succeeded by sheer guts in overcoming the tragedy of Ken's total blindness.

The author has succeeded in producing the best description I have ever read of the work carried out by the only troops in the British Army who were always on active service – the Bomb Disposal companies of the Royal Engineers. While most of us were training in the United Kingdom and preparing for the invasion of Europe, Bomb Disposal units were busy with their dangerous craft in which almost daily they matched their skill and nerve against the inventive genius of the German scientists.

Ken Revis was training to be a structural engineer and had almost qualified when the last war broke out. He joined up and, at the age of 23, was commissioned in the Royal Engineers, and was posted to Bomb Disposal. On 1 March 1941, he married Jo. During the next two years he dealt with many different types of bomb, showing nerve, courage, and organizing ability in the process.

Then in 1943 his unit was ordered to 'delouse' Brighton piers. At 10 a.m. on 10 September 1943, while he was removing booby-traps from the West Pier, thirteen mines suddenly blew up in his face. The mangled body of Ken Revis was rushed to East Grinstead Hospital, where a long, hard trail lay in front of him, for it required no less than twenty skilled plastic operations to remake Ken's shattered face and body, but not even the most highly skilled specialist could replace his eyes; so, after some weeks in hospital he was told the dread news that he would never see again. This was the turning point.

It would have been so easy to give way, but not the Revises. With single-minded courage the two of them – because a blinded man and his wife form one team – refused to accept blindness. They were determined to lead an independent, normal life again. And on 3 January 1944, Ken arrived at Church Stretton, the war-time home of St Dunstan's, that remarkable organization which in the course of two world wars has cared for over 5,000 war-blinded Servicemen from all over the Commonwealth. This was the beginning. He learned braille, typing, and many other things. He took part in dances and even ran in the sports there. He was just the type to absorb and benefit from the spirit of St Dunstan's.

His first job – arranged by Sir Ian (now Lord) Fraser – was to be assistant to Sir Clutha Mackenzie, the head of St Dunstan's in India. After Indian independence the Revises returned home. Once more Sir Ian stepped in and arranged for Ken to be appointed to the personnel department of the Nuffield Group at Cowley – an organization with a magnificent record for helping war-disabled men.

It was here that a third member was added to the Revis team, a white Alsatian guide dog called Sandra, who became Ken's inseparable companion.

But even this was not enough. Ken felt that he must have some proper professional qualification: he is the type of man who never stands still. He decided, therefore, to become a solicitor. His firm gave him leave of absence, and St Dunstan's, as always, helped with his studies; now, after five years' solid work, he is a qualified solicitor and assistant Press officer back at Nuffield's.

That is the work side of the picture, but I doubt whether any other totally blind man has ever succeeded in leading such a full life. He has raised hundreds of pounds to help in the training of Guide Dogs, has piloted a glider, water-skied, driven an MGA at 100 miles an hour on an airfield runway, ridden horses, sung on television, and learned to play musical instruments – a truly wonderful record.

This foreword is already too long. My only excuse is that I have been carried away by the Revis story. Even so I cannot finish without paying a tribute to Jo, without whom Ken, with all his courage, could not possibly have triumphed over adversity in the way he has.

I am left with the conviction that the characters of these two young people have been strengthened by the struggle they have been through.

Black Rod's Office,
House of Lords,
November 1961

Chapter 1

EARLY EXPLOSIONS

"Shall I ever see again?" The question throbbed through his brain as the bandages hid his eyes in those first fateful days. Shall I ever see? Ken Revis lay in the end bed of the ward at East Grinstead, the one nearest the Sister's small room. They kept this position for the most serious cases, so that she could get to it quickly.

He remembered the pier. And the crash. Nothing more. Everything was dark, and he could not change it. A tight, singing sensation hurt his head. As well as the pain in his head and shoulders, his left arm lay limp.

He knew he had been blown up, but he did not know how much damage had been done. Even his wife Jo did not know exactly what he was like or what had happened on that nightmare night after the accident.

A pulp of blood in the shape of a head: that was his featureless face. He had a large number of deep, extensive wounds to his forehead, eyes, nose, and upper lids. Many of the wounds went right down to the bones. The skull lay bare on his forehead. The left-cheek gash gored into the sinus. His mouth had been torn; his nose distended.

Worst of all, both eyes were badly battered. The corneas had been ripped; the globes bled.

Smaller wounds to the lower lip and chin, but still bad. And the rest of the body, too. Many superficial wounds were over the front of his chest, one on the left shoulder; injuries peppered his left arm; he had a fractured left wrist; multiple abrasions on knees and elsewhere.

Ken went into the operating theatre at about 8 p.m. Hours of urgent plastic surgery lay ahead. The surgeons explored every single wound, removed all the dirt, and took out the dead tissue. They turned to the two biggest facial wounds: the forehead and left cheek. The great gash exposing the skull was sewn up. They actually opened out the

1

cheek, and held it there with two long 'forks' while they fished for and removed loose bits of bone from the sinus deep in the cheek. Blood ran as the clock on the wall raced round towards midnight. The swollen nose and lacerated lips had their turn, yet Ken's face was still carved with cruel marks. But the eyes – what of them? The surgeons trimmed off bits of tissue protruding through them, and repaired the globes as best as they could. And as Ken had lost a lot of his eyelids, they performed the preliminary skin-graft with moulds fitted over the eyes during this eyelid surgery. There was no time to talk about prospects, but everyone in the theatre knew that the hope for his sight was very slender. The eyes themselves were not removed.

Midnight. Ken's arms and other affected parts were repaired as well, and both big and small wounds cleaned up carefully and dressed. Amazingly enough, apart from a perforated eardrum caused by the blast, Ken hardly had any serious subsequent trouble, and the surgery began to heal almost at once.

But the big question still remained to haunt him through those days and weeks after the operation. *Shall I ever see again?*

He lay there, waiting and wondering. In the darkness of day-time, as well as night, there was too much time to wonder about an uncertain future. Even with Jo beside him. Outside the ward the world went on around the little low-built cottage hospital that had already become synonymous with plastic surgery. The sprawling ward blocks, the lawns leading down to the road, and the road winding away into the town. All these went unknown to Ken. Even the ward itself meant no more than a succession of sounds. So sometimes he found himself turning inevitably inward, away from the world and his own future.

Slowly the gnawing question of his sight merged into his mother's voice, echoing from the depths of his memory:

"Will it blow up, dear?"

He seemed to hear her asking again the question she was always asking in response to his boyhood inventions. He tried to recall the first time she had used the phrase, which became one of the Revis family jokes. It must have been over the gunpowder at home back in Bedford.

Ken found a recipe for making gunpowder in a book, with alarming ingredients like saltpetre, sulphur, and carbon. To mix these better, he added water and then slid a tray of the smooth, dark grey paste into the lighted gas oven to dry. Luckily, he retrieved it before the moisture had gone completely, and Mrs Revis never knew how near they had come to being blown up!

Armed with this half-dry explosive, however, Ken proceeded at once to try to make his own brand of fireworks. He filled a long cardboard box with the compound, and stuck several blank cartridges into it, forming a row along the top of the box. He hoped to produce a series of small explosions from one cartridge to another.

Ken took the box outside into the garden and stood it on the wooden seat. A fuse was the next necessity, so he soaked a piece of blotting-paper in saltpetre, tucked it into one end of the home-made pyrotechnic, lit it – and retired rapidly.

The flagstone garden was almost totally enclosed, so the instantaneous roar when the charge went off echoed deafeningly between the house and the garden walls. Ken glimpsed a large charred dent in the surface of the seat. That was the end of fireworks.

When he was ten, he won a scholarship to Bedford School, which he joined in the winter term of 1928. This was a new world, and he felt lost and alone for a few days as he looked over the rail and into the pit of the huge hall.

He soon fitted into the school scheme, however, and at home continued his individual experiments in chemistry. This time they took the form of balloons. Ken decided to fill them with hydrogen gas and release them with a label attached, hopefully asking finders to return the balloons to him. One half-filled specimen was suddenly blown out of his hands, swept straight up the chimney by the draught of the fire, and appeared over the rooftops before falling to earth again.

His very first filled and labelled balloon rose triumphantly from the garden, floated southward, and vanished over the outskirts of Bedford. A week later, Ken was excited to get a letter from forty miles away, enclosing the shreds of rubber.

The balloon game palled after a time, and he started to wonder what else he could do with hydrogen. Then he read the fact that "hydrogen burns with a blue flame," and decided to prove the point. He used a wide-necked hard-glass bottle containing zinc and fitted with a rubber bung and tube. Ken poured in pungent spirits of salts and quickly replaced the bung. The acid started to act at once, and the zinc dissolved in a flurry of foam – the heat burning a brown ring on the kitchen table.

The experiment had barely begun yet, though. By now, the gas was hissing out of the tube, not pure hydrogen but a mixture of hydrogen and air. When Ken applied a light to it, he saw no blue flame. Instead, the whole bottle shattered, covering his face and shoulders with splintered glass, acid, and scraps of corroding zinc. Luckily, they missed his eyes, and he groped a way to the kitchen sink to swamp his stinging face and neck with water to wash away the burning chemicals. No wonder Mrs Revis used to ask, "Will it blow up, dear?"

3

Ken's work with his hands at school took the more familiar forms of carpentry, machine-shop sessions, and forging such unlikely objects as meat-hooks. And in his workshop at home, he developed a passionate devotion for aircraft, making models of every kind. He became proficient at recognition, too, and with the world of aeronautics still young, there was an added zest in pointing up in the sky and telling a friend, "That's a Bristol Bulldog Mark Two."

Soon he talked of little else but aircraft, and wrote to every manufacturer in the country asking for details of their planes. In response they sent him catalogues, glossy prints, and plans of many planes. Ken went a stage farther, too, by writing to German firms like Dornier, Heinkel, and Focke-Wulf.

His early efforts at making models proved to be rather crude, shaped from the slats of old Venetian blinds no longer used at home. Later he graduated to scale models, carved from the solid wood and based on drawings. Ken always rounded them off by painting their correct international colours.

Shall I ever see again?

Perhaps his eyes were fated from the start. After the gunpowder plot and his hydrogen bomb – what came next? Lying in his bed at East Grinstead, he decided it must have been the bar-bells. These became quite a craze as he went in for body-building exercises at home, with the aid of dumbbells, a spring chest-expander, and even a rowing machine.

For sheer ingenuity, it would be hard to beat the pair of bar-bells he made. First, he found a couple of seven-pound tea-chests, which he filled with concrete, and then he embedded an old gas-pipe four feet long between the two, and allowed the concrete to harden. When it had set solid, he stripped the chests off – and there was a pair of bar-bells. With this home-made apparatus he performed every kind of strengthening exercise he could think of, picking them off the floor and heaving them above his head in the best circus traditions.

But the day came when he lay on the bedroom floor and started to raise them while still keeping flat. Somehow, they slipped through Ken's hands and crashed onto his face. Full length on the floor, he was unable to get out of the way in time, and the gas-pipe hit him squarely across the eyes and stunned him. One of his cheeks was gashed and bleeding badly, and he could not see for nearly an hour. Gradually his sight seemed to return, but for a while after that he felt cross-eyed, as the bedroom reeled around in front of him.

Ken's parents were out at the time, and he felt so stupid about the accident that he decided to make an excuse to them. It was only a white lie after all, so he told them, "I ran into the cycle shed putting my bike away."

It seemed almost as if Ken was fated to be blinded. When a fourth accident happened Ken could have been excused for thinking there must be some conspiracy against him, though he had to admit that they were all his own fault.

From fireworks and model planes, Ken was graduating to bigger things. He heard that a local scrap-metal merchant had a complete motor-cycle for sale in his yard, so Ken and a friend hurried over there as soon as they could. Looking beyond the maze of mangles, prams, and bedsteads, they suddenly saw it. A 1923-model 2¾-h.p. Douglas bike, its twin cylinders rusty, its paintwork peeling, its wheel rims sunken into two worn and flat tyres. None of this mattered to Ken, for the only part actually missing was the top of the carburettor, while the throttle-cable, which should have led to it, hung lifelessly across the dented petrol-tank.

Ken had never felt more excited as he proudly pushed the old machine out of the yard in the direction of home, having paid the full price the dealer asked for it – precisely half a crown!

At home, however, the machine aroused almost complete lack of enthusiasm. Undismayed, Ken kept it reverently in the cycle shed, and soon started the job of rejuvenation. First of all, he had to remove the whole engine from the frame to handle it easily in his little cellar workshop. Meticulously he dismantled, inspected, cleaned, reassembled, and refitted to the frame, so that at last came the moment for actual testing. Ken chose a day when all the family were at home, and announced:

"Could you spare a few minutes if I bring the bike into the scullery?"

Before anyone could answer, he had wheeled the Douglas into Mrs Revis's red-tiled scullery and was summoning his parents and sister Marjorie. By the time they had crowded into the little room, with the bike sprawled diagonally across it, scarcely a spare inch remained. Ken stood the bike on its back stand, pointing it so that the rear wheel was near the open door.

By this time the family began to be more interested as Ken assigned a job to each of them, although his mother and sister were still apprehensive. Mr Revis had to hold on to the handlebars in case the engine started unexpectedly and shook the machine from the safety of its stand. Since no proper petrol connexion existed between the tank and the carburettor, Marjorie held a glass chemistry funnel, filled with petrol and linked by a rubber tube to the underside of the carburettor. And in the absence of a throttle control, to Mrs Revis went the job of holding the throttle cable, with instructions to keep it in the quarter-open position. Ken himself had to haul away on the back wheel to turn the engine over, since the bike had no kick start or clutch, and so could not have both wheels on the floor at the vital moment without running forward.

"Now are you all ready?" Ken made sure. Then he flooded the carburettor and ran round to the rear of the machine. Grabbing the tyre, he heaved slowly; the belt took up the drive, and the engine turned over, protesting in a series of hisses. Ken pulled strongly on the tyre, but it gasped and stopped. Again, he pulled, again the gasp and a little cough from the carburettor. Marjorie nearly dropped the funnel in fright. One more pull, and the engine exploded into life with a crackle that filled the whole scullery with sound, while the two short exhaust-pipes belched black smoke over everything – and everyone. There was no stopping it now, as the bike began to shake with excitement at its own success. Despite the smoke and the smell, the family held on gamely to their handlebars, funnel, and cable as Ken beamed at them through the fog. But the funnelful of petrol could not last long, and in another minute the engine spluttered to a stand-still after its deafening debut in the scullery.

The Douglas did not yet have any mudguards or number plates. These details, plus the fact that Ken was not yet sixteen, made riding on roads out of the question. But behind the house stood a strip of grassland simply made for use as a dirt-track, so with a school friend who had paid all of five shillings for his particular bike, Ken raced round to his heart's content. They loved their hours on this track, adjusting, repairing, revving up, and racing.

Ken noticed petrol leaking from his square tank one day, so stopped using the bike till he could solder it secure again. He dutifully drained the tank, and then left it a clear day for the vapour to evaporate completely. To try to expel any remnant of petrol vapour, he blew through the filler hole before approaching the tank with the soldering iron. Ken brought the head of the hot iron towards the tank; there was a flash of vapour, the tank exploded, and its seams split open. A tongue of flame from the vapour spat up at him, singeing his eyebrows and hair. But once again his eyes were all right.

By the time that Ken heard he had matriculated, he and his parents had decided that civil engineering seemed to be the best profession for him, so early in the New Year of 1935 he was articled to the county surveyor of Bedfordshire.

Gradually he grew familiar with the precision instruments of surveying, both inside the drawing-office and out in the field. Blueprints, set-squares, protractors, and all the rest of the draughtsman's equipment that needed keen eyes and mind; and on the road and bridges of Bedfordshire, he grappled with theodolites, levelling-staff, coloured ranging-rods, tape, marking-pegs, chalk, and a dumpy level.

Ken might recall the summer of 1935 as the start of his studies, but he was much likelier to connect it with the arrival of his very first car. An old friend found a dilapidated 1926 Rover at a dealers in Coventry, and the vehicle had to be towed from there to Bromham, the village three miles from Bedford, where the Revis family had now built a house.

"Thanks terribly, Fitz," Ken said when he saw the car, "she's absolutely super."

What he saw was not, in fact, the old wreck before him but the nucleus of a smart sports car. At the end of the month, the engine lay literally in pieces, and the chassis shivered naked except for the front scuttle and instrument panel. Ken managed to get some necessary new parts for the engine, which he revitalized and returned to the frame. Although the car still had no body or even mudguards, he could not resist trying it out, and the engine responded to the starting-handle and with a series of faltering explosions. The second time Ken cranked it, the engine really got going, and as the short exhaust-pipe was shorn of its silencer it woke up the village with a machine-gun burst of noise.

Ken hopped round to the steering-wheel and put a board across the chassis for a seat. Since no floorboards existed yet to which the throttle linkage could be attached, he controlled the carburettor opening with a piece of soft wire bound around his foot! The engine responded well to the waggle of Ken's foot, and an occasional orange flame flickered from the end of the exhaust-pipe by his legs. But the main thing was that it went. Next Ken had the detail of making the body of the car.

Five-ply wood formed the unconventional material for the body, and Ken added a canvas hood and a tonneau cover fastening over the luggage space at the rear. Starting from scratch, he was able to create just the dashing design of bodywork he wanted for a racy look. He decided to stick to the original rear mudguards, but replace the front ones, which would have been quite unsuitable for the streamlined shape he had in mind. Fitz finally came to the rescue and persuaded a friend in the sheet-metal industry to have a pair rolled to measure, and when these at length came down from Coventry the car at once assumed the breed of a racer.

This impression Ken confirmed by the fold-flat windscreen and outsize steering-wheel. Not being the superstitious sort, Ken procured the wheel from a crashed Italian racing-car that had no further use for a sense of direction. To carry the thing off completely, however, every detail had to be right, so Ken made sure that the gear-lever became as short and stumpy as in the cars that tore round Brooklands. The paintwork put on with loving care had the official identity of British racing green, and for that final master-touch, the undersides of the mudguards, as well as the chassis – for the most part exposed – were in the contrast of bright red.

All that remained now was for Ken to christen the car, which he did. The name read Dorcas II, after some legendary soul who had been "full of good works." Ken reckoned that the Rover was worth that title too!

His life during those three years' training was really wrapped up in his cars, for towards the end of the period he changed the green-and-red Rover for a Riley, which he bought at the then considerable price of £24. He did less to this one than to Dorcas II, but brightened its colour by painting the bonnet and mudguards cream to create a sophisticated two-tone of chocolate and cream. When Ken left home for an engineering job in Reading, it was the Riley that took him the seventy miles or so to his new workplace.

After the first few days' strangeness, Ken began to revel in his independence, especially as Jack Hamer, in the same house, was as keen on cars as he was. Looking down the columns of a motoring journal, an advertisement caught Ken's eye that summer of 1938, and he drove over to Windsor to the address given. There he saw and fell for a two-litre open four-seater Lagonda, which he got for £40. With the engine positively purring as he eventually drove it back to Reading, Ken's life seemed brimming. Not to be outdone by this move, Jack appeared within a fortnight with another two-litre Lagonda – but one year newer than Ken's!

Most of Ken's work while he stayed at Reading was taken up with the reconstruction of Loddon Bridge between the town and Wokingham, and he naturally spent most of his days on the site. From the bridge, Ken could not avoid seeing the Service and civilian planes on their way to and from near-by Woodley aerodrome and, in fact, they taxied close to the garden of the Falcon Inn, where he and Jack used to have a drink after the day's work.

Woodley was an R.A.F. Volunteer Reserve (R.A.F.V.R.) centre, and its promise of weekend flying training decided Ken to join. He got as far as receiving all the sheaf of papers, filling them in, and even having a stringent medical examination. The recent memory of Munich made him want to be prepared in case a war should start. However, he was destined not to join the R.A.F.V.R. About the same time, in April 1939, as he had finished all these formalities he applied also for a good job in Lincolnshire. The post was engineering assistant in the county surveyor's department at Sleaford, county town of Kesteven, one of the three administrative divisions of Lincolnshire.

He got the job.

As the Lagonda nosed into the sleepy main street of Sleaford, known as Southgate, Ken sensed slight misgivings, but as soon as he settled into the White Horse there, he felt his surroundings had become friendlier, more familiar. Southgate formed the spine of the town, with a level-crossing at the south end and small market-square to the north.

So, Sleaford was the setting for Ken's last idyllic summer before the war, when he had only recently reached his twenty-first birthday and his life seemed to stretch ahead as one endless adventure. He had a special reason for remembering Southgate, too, for he was steering the Lagonda through the narrowest section of the street, with houses and shops built up closely on either side, when he saw a gorgeous girl with large eyes standing on the nearside pavement. Ken was compelled to turn round for a moment as he passed her, and almost ran the car on to the pavement in so doing, as the street curved slightly to the right. He jerked the wheel in time, but it was too late, and the road too narrow, to try and stop to see her again.

The next day he did see her, though, again by chance. She was sitting at the driving-wheel of a car with a lady whom Ken took to be her mother, and a small girl in pigtails who could well have been her sister. Their car stood parked near the council offices, and as Ken walked past it to go inside, they really saw each other for the first time. He knew he must meet her, and could not think of much else till he had found out more about her and how it could be arranged.

In an office of men, it did not turn out to be too hard to discover – in as casual a way as he could – the name of such a striking girl. By a coincidence that seemed almost inevitable, Ken learned that she would be at "a friend of a friend's" party that evening. It took only a small favour for Ken to be invited too. The rest of the day seemed endless as he lingered on in the prospect of meeting Joan, as her name was.

One look round the room, and Ken saw she was there.

"Shall we dance?"

For the rest of that evening, they completely forgot their friends, the house, everything. The only detail in their way was that Jo happened to be engaged at the time! After that midsummer-night meeting – still vivid twenty-two years later – they "pretty well fell for each other from then on," as Ken told his mother, and in fact he took Jo home to Bedford to meet his parents the weekend war was declared.

Ken was working for Part "A" of his Final A.M.I.C.E. (Associate Member of the Institution of Civil Engineers), but he would never take it now. When they got back to the bustle of market-day in Sleaford Ken and Jo went round to the tennis club for a game, but things did not seem quite the same. The summer was over, though they still had each other.

Ken came down to breakfast one morning that September to find a letter from the Institution of Civil Engineers recommending him to apply for a commission in the Royal Engineers. Ken read down the list of reception units throughout the country, and found that the one at Cambridge University would be the nearest for him. He had already decided to join up in some capacity, and so he told the office he would be taking the day off, and drove down through the flat expanses of East Anglia to the spiky spires of Cambridge.

At the University Reception Unit, he parked the Lagonda, and in a few minutes found himself undergoing a stiff medical. Eyesight, hearing, and general health were all A.1., and so Ken took the oath of allegiance to Our Sovereign Lord the King, from which moment he became 2192852 Sapper Revis, K.C.

Ken bounced out of the ceremony, pleased that he had taken the plunge, and treated himself to a scalding lunch of curry at an Indian restaurant in Cambridge.

Back at Sleaford once more, Ken lived through a period of mixed emotions. He wanted to get into the war – civil defence duties were no substitute – but both he and Jo knew that this would mean parting. They made the most of the "phoney war" months that winter, and saw each other most evenings.

His landlady came into the dining-room one morning to pour out his coffee for breakfast, and even she had noticed their late nights.

"Mr Revis," she said, solemn-faced, "you'll be an old man by the time you're thirty!"

Ken only smiled as he gulped down the coffee and went to work.

The nearest the war came to Sleaford was when a stick of bombs burst on the R.A.F. station at Cranwell, five miles away. This incident only served to remind Ken how impatient he was to be part of it all, and he felt a certain indefinable fascination for what the war held in store for him.

At last, the posting notice came, but before he went, he gave Jo an engagement ring on 1 March 1940. Then he threw one or two oddments into an old suitcase, pulled on his leather coat, set his check cap at a jaunty angle, and went to war. In fact, this meant taking the train a mere twenty miles to Newark, where he stepped on to the platform to see an untidy knot of young men all clustered round an R.E. corporal. From the moment he reached them, he was really in the Army at last.

10

And if it had not dawned on him already, the corporal's comment on the march to the barracks would have brought it home:

"Stop talking there. You're in the Army now."

After twenty minutes' march, they wheeled into the dirty forecourt of a building that they learned was the barracks. As it was now nearly evening, they looked forward to a meal, so after the issue of tin plates they joined the food queue quite eagerly.

They received an adequate if unimaginative meal of stew and rice-pudding, but one thing seemed to be missing. They had to manage without any knife, fork, or spoon! Eating without eating irons. Ken rose to the occasion, as he was hungry by this time, shovelling the food with his penknife in one hand and a thick slice of bread in the other!

Ken and the others were all billeted out in private houses, one to each family, and as he put on his battledress blouse in the little bedroom next morning, he looked in the mirror to see its collar jutting forward like the prow of a boat, leaving a whole expanse of throat and neck exposed. Like many recruits, he had to visit the regimental tailor subsequently for an alteration. But that first day the collar stood out with a will of its own. Ken pouched his trousers carefully over webbing gaiters, placed his Service cap at the correct slant, and stepped out into the little Newark street.

There on the other side stood a fair-haired, pink-complexioned boy he had spoken to the previous night – John Price by name – and at the sight of each other for the first time in uniform, they both burst out laughing and set off for the barracks. Ken and John joined the rest of the recruits forming three ranks for drill, and, glancing along their lines, Ken could not help grinning at the shaggy-haired, precariously capped, and floppy-trousered one-night-old soldiers – including himself. After sixteen days' drill on that same square, his first pair of thick black boots were worn through.

Field work followed the drill square, carried out for the most part on Beacon Hill, the site of a disused brickyard. Among many other things there, they had one memorable trench-digging task timed to start at midnight and continue through torrential rain for four hours. Between the third and fourth hours, some of the party got so soaked, frozen, and miserable that they nearly launched an open revolt on the young officer in charge of them.

The weeks went by quickly, punctuated only by such incidents as an enormous rat which ran over Ken as he slept on the floor of the schoolroom where they stayed later. Before fourteen weeks were up at Newark, Ken had been promoted to temporary acting unpaid lance-corporal, together with John Price and several of the others. They hoped

11

this meant that they would be posted to an Officer Cadet Training Unit (O.C.T.U.) Then, sure enough, at midsummer the posting came, just a year after Ken and Jo had met for the first time at that wonderful party in Sleaford. Like everyone else in Britain then, Ken wondered what another year would bring, but he was too excited about the prospect of the officers' course to worry. The next six months would be occupied with this training, anyway, which would be a full-time job if he were to pass out successfully.

One of the first things John Price and Ken did when they reached Aldershot was to unpick the chevrons from their battledress blouses and greatcoats, to be replaced by the distinctive white shoulder-flashes and bands round their caps. But in case they got any premature ideas above their rank, Sergeant Singleton entered. An impeccable, young-looking class sergeant, he proceeded to instruct them how to lay out their webbing equipment in the barrack-room and how to fold their blankets so that the alignment could easily be checked from the doorway. He then added with a suggestion of a smile, "There'll be trouble for any gentleman disobeying these orders."

So, it started: infantry training, mechanical transport, explosives and demolitions, bridging, water-supply, and others. And at the end of each three-week section on these subjects there was a 'browning-off' parade. This meant a ticking-off from the commanding officer for bad work in either practice or the written examination, which ended each section of the course. These browning-off parades came to be dreaded, as at every one some unlucky cadet was "RTUed" – returned to unit. As this happened regularly, and the beds in each room had to be evenly spaced to fill the floor, the remaining cadets found themselves enlarging the intervals between each bed until there was an alarming desert of floor free.

As the Battle of Britain progressed, they used to look towards London and could see the tracer bullets breaking the night sky with ribbons of fire. A stick of bombs actually straddled the barracks once, which may have given rise to rumour that those who had completed half the course were to be commissioned immediately as infantry officers – in view of the serious situation of the war.

Like most rumours, this one proved false, and the course continued. A prominent purpose of the course was to produce and maintain a high degree of physical fitness in junior officers, and in Ken's time at Aldershot he thought himself lucky to have Alf Gover, the Surrey and England cricketer, in charge of him. Gover went elsewhere during the course, however, and they all felt sorry until his place was taken by another well-known cricketer, Denis Compton.

12

They found their regular duties toughening, too, as they dug and revetted miles of deep anti-tank ditches across that part of the country at a time when an enemy invasion was most likely. Pick, shovel, axe, and wire-cutters they used to gash out these protective ditches, and then with winter came bridge-building under the critical eye of Major "Bags of Dash" Browning. This culminated in a night-bridging exercise, for which they were driven in trucks through the darkness to a spot in a farmyard. After unloading box girders and other heavy gear for the bridge, Ken and some of the others stood several hours waist-deep in water until dawn. Then while the others rested, Ken and another cadet decided to have a run along the river-bank to try to warm themselves up a bit. A quarter of a mile they trotted in the grey November light, when rising right in front of them stood Loddon Bridge, which Ken had supervised. He had no idea they were near it, and as he looked at its familiar form, that pre-war world suddenly seemed gone for ever.

Eventually the course was over, and one of the first serious signs of commissioning came when representatives of the local military tailors invaded the barrack-room to take orders for officers' uniforms.

More than the new uniform, perhaps, Ken felt most pleased with his Sam Browne belt. He managed to get a golden-brown tone instead of the too-frequent boiled-beetroot colour, and he spent a lot of time polishing it around the curved surface of a barrack-room litter-bin, till it shone more like burnished copper than brown leather. Boots, belts, and buttons, all received affectionate attention in those final few days before the passing-out parade, which took all their concentration after six months' slogging for it.

So, when Ken glanced at a typewritten sheet on the notice-board over Christmas and read their postings, his destination did not do more than raise average interest in him. The riotous Christmas had already arrived; the passing-out parade would follow within forty-eight hours; and he read the postings casually. He and John Price were to join Bomb Disposal.

28 December dawned, and the class strode on to the main square with everything ashine – including their faces. Sergeant Singleton spoke some whispered words of good-humoured encouragement before calling them to attention and marching them to the centre. They stood there motionless, in perfect formation, rifles sloped to the sky, only waiting for the next shouted command.

But a breeze had sprung up! Across the width of the square, the cadet officer taking them jerked his body taut, opened his mouth, and gave the word. The class listened intently, but only a wavering sound reached them. Some ordered arms. Some presented arms. They had

13

bungled it badly through no fault of their own. The moment passed, however, and soon they were marching briskly off the square, cursing yet commissioned in the Corps of Royal Engineers.

By eleven o'clock, Ken and a colleague, Ray Rogerson, were near the guardroom wearing their uniforms self-consciously. They felt embarrassed at returning salutes from other ranks who had no need to 'throw one up' to them the day before, and greeting junior officers, whom they would have saluted, with a feeble smile!

Then up to Sleaford for a wonderful few days' leave. Ken had not seen Jo for months, and his parents were there, too. Ray's home was nearby, so Ken and Jo joined Ray and his girlfriend at a New Year's Eve ball. This night went down as another milestone in Ken's life. The only flaw to the whole leave was when he had to tell his mother about his new posting. Now that he had thought about it, Ken felt more excited than apprehensive, perhaps partly because he still knew nothing at all about German bombs.

He pacified his mother by telling her that he would have to go on a bomb-disposal training course first anyway, adding, "And don't worry – I don't expect I'll ever have to handle any live ones."

He did not know whether Mrs Revis believed it or not, but he had done his best to put her at ease. As for Ken, he felt that his personal war would soon be starting.

Chapter 2

KEN'S FIRST BOMB

The train reached the rainswept blacked-out station at Haywards Heath on the early evening of 6 January 1941, and a truck took Ken to his company. As he sat beside the driver in the dark cab, the letters "BD", for Bomb Disposal, stood out on the windscreen, and although they were swishing through the streets of the town on a depressing night, Ken felt suddenly proud. It was inevitable that he would be attracted by the glamour of the dangerous job ahead, but, deeper than that, the sense of belonging was born in him again.

"I'm Kenway. You'd better come in and meet the O.C. [Officer Commanding]; we're just going to start dinner."

As well as Major Martin, Ken met Captain Grey, Lieutenant Tyson, and John Price, whom he had left at the passing-out parade ten days earlier. An enormous log fire flickered in the stone fireplace of Mallows, this large house that was the officers' mess. And in the course of the week, Ken learned three interesting things: (1) he could put up a second pip at once to become Lieutenant Kenneth Revis, (2) he would be going on the bomb-disposal course almost at once, and (3) on his return he would be posted to a detachment at Battle, in Sussex, to command his first section.

Ken went down to Melksham, in Wiltshire, with John Price for the course, and met several old friends from O.C.T.U. at once. On that night before they began the course, they felt a mingling of joy, excitement, apprehension, and determination, all of which seemed to be intensified by another storm swept night. Five of them shared a hut. And if they could have known, they had reason for their emotions, because of the five, two were later killed and one badly injured. Those were the sort of odds in bomb disposal at that time.

Next day they met "the mad chemist," as the previous class had nicknamed the chief instructor, and from then on, they had no time to think of anything except bombs – and how to tackle them. Ken realized that his chance of survival probably depended to a considerable extent on what he learned here, for the first mistake in this job was frequently the last. So, he listened eagerly to the introduction to the subject.

Bombs commonly failed to explode at once either intentionally or through a fault. Whichever was the case, Bomb Disposal had the job of making them harmless before any damage could be done. When a bomb was in its first few inches of flight from an aircraft, electric current was switched on, and by means of a light metal sliding connexion a charge was given to an electric condenser in the bomb's fuse. While the bomb fell this electric charge remained stored in the condenser, and on impact with the target, a delicate trembler switch operated to detonate the bomb. If it incorporated a delayed-action device the explosion would not occur until the time had elapsed.

The current released from the condenser caused heat to be generated in a wire. This ignited a match-head substance which, in turn, caused the first detonation of a chain. The gaine, as this was called, next detonated a large pellet of picric acid in the exploder pocket of the bomb, which fired the main charge. Fuses were generally inserted in the side of the bomb and secured with a locking ring, with the markings and electrical connexions clearly visible.

At the end of the first morning, Ken had filled several pages of an exercise book. He represented a fuse-head by pencilling around a penny, inking inside the circle the appropriate symbols. Then he listed the fuse-head markings and the latest way of discharging the current for all the fuses that were then known to be in use.

As the course progressed, Ken learned details of the different bombs being dropped by the Germans, ranging from 50 kilograms (kg), or about 1 cwt., to 250 kg, 500 kg, and 1000 kg – about a ton. Bigger than that were Esau, 1400 kg, and Satan, 1800 kg.

Once having learned the basic problem of U.X.B.s – the universal name for unexploded bombs – Ken began to get an idea of the ingenious ways in which scientists were combating it. Then, as the enemy realized later that their bombs were being dismantled without exploding, they introduced more complications which called for fresh measures from Bomb Disposal.

The electric charge stored by the tiny condenser in the fuse could often be dissipated by applying a small metal cap by hand to the fuse-head; this had projections corresponding to the sprung electrical studs on the head of the fuse itself. But this elementary method sometimes set off the bomb instead of rendering it safe, so another way had to be found.

By attaching a specially shaped cap with a tube to the fuse-head, an electrolytic fluid could be injected through the plungers into the body of the fuse, so that the charge would gradually flow from the condenser, through the conducting liquid, to the bomb-case, and so to earth. The trembler switch would then be unable to launch its lightning chain of detonation.

Far more frightening, however, was the introduction by the enemy of delayed-action fuses, with the dreaded clockwork 17 fuse. The psychological effect of bombs that might go off hours – even days – after being dropped was great, so an answer had to be found to the 17 fuse.

In the early days Bomb Disposal carried in their equipment ordinary medical stethoscopes! But later on, an electric stethoscope with a magnetic microphone and a headset came into service, so that it was sometimes possible – before actually reaching the bomb – to press a metal probe into the ground beneath the excavation so far made, locate the bomb, and use the stethoscope on the upper end of the probe to listen for the clock. If it were not ticking this could mean either that the particular bomb had no clockwork fuse, or that it did contain a clock which would restart with or without any movement or vibration. One antidote to the 17 fuse was the clock-stopper, a heavy electro-magnet which normally proved effective in ruining any possibility of the clock starting. But as it was so bulky, it could not always be used.

Another way of stopping 17 clocks was to drill the fuse-head and inject into it a fairly stiff mixture of dental cement and water, so that when it hardened it would clog the moving parts of the sensitive clockwork mechanism.

Every eventuality had to be considered. Sometimes, for one reason or another, the bomb just could not be made safe or removed to a remote spot to be exploded. To meet this case, the sterilizer would be brought into action to steam out the main explosive charge of the bomb. This unreal-looking equipment consisted basically of a boiler carried by truck which could be manhandled on the site by several men with long carrying poles! The boiler supplied the steam, and a long pipe fed it into a delicate revolving device that could be clamped on to the bomb.

Operated by steam pressure, this trepanned a large hole in the case of the bomb, through which the pipe was passed. The revolving nozzle of the pipe then melted the crystalline high explosive and forced the molten result back through a flexible metal outer covering to the steam hose, for collection and safe detonation on hardening. The heat, smell, and general dirtiness of the boiler made the sterilizer rather an unpopular monster, especially as its cloud of hissing steam usually had to be endured at the bottom of a bomb-shaft already short of fresh air.

The course concluded with a practical test in bomb disposal. Ken and the others had to dig a shaft to discover and dismantle a bomb buried about fifteen feet below ground by the instructors. This was a test of everything they had been taught, including correctly timbering the excavation. Ken's engineering training had already taught him the need for supporting the sides of a shaft strongly against the lateral force of the soil.

The exercise rather deteriorated into farce, however, for the thought of burrowing for a planted bomb would not have excited them under ideal conditions, but on the day fixed for the start of the operation the weather was terrible. Rain had been pattering on the roof of their lecture hut throughout the course, making the site ankle-deep in mud. Under actual circumstances, this would have washed out the hole of entry of the bomb and its direction – both so vital to know before searching for a U.X.B. – but they set to work, digging at the spot shown them.

The rain streamed down over everything, and they soon had to use pumps to cope with the waterlogged ground. But even with these, the mud started to slide inward when they tried to timber the shaft. Soaked, shivering, and plastered with mud, they dug and timbered till they got down to the bomb the following afternoon. Then they went through the motions of discharging the current and withdrawing its fuse, so that they could race off into hot baths and dry uniforms.

A day or so later Ken found himself on the road between Battle and Hastings, where at the top of the hill, half a mile or so from the ancient abbey, stands Glengorse. This lovely mansion in wooded grounds had been taken over by a Bomb Disposal detachment, and Walker was the subaltern in charge of one of its two sections, while Ken led the other.

Walker wasted no time, as they had several bombs on their books needing attention. He took Ken to a pleasant avenue in Hastings where a bomb had dived into a garden only a yard or so from the footpath. Walker introduced Ken to Sergeant French, and formally handed over the section to his command. Already Ken felt aware of the mixture of excitement and apprehension, but he had no time yet to dwell longer on personal reactions.

Then he saw the bomb. It had deposited its four-bladed tail almost intact within two feet of the surface, and the thing had already been identified as a 500-kg. Most of the work of exposing had been done, and it only remained to scrape away about eighteen inches more earth from the centre to uncover the fuse.

The fuse-head gleamed up at him, its two electric connexions staring like evil eyes. Ken lay down beside the bomb as best he could, with his legs braced against the side of the hole. The fuse-head was covered with the kind of engraved and stamped marking he had been taught to recognize. The main mark he made out read "15" in a small circle. According to the drill, this should be the kind of fuse that could be discharged by earthing its charge with a cap placed in position for a number of seconds.

"This is it. This is the real thing. Must remember everything I learned last week. No need to worry. It's such a big bomb – if it doesn't go off, I'm all right, if it does go off, I won't know a thing about it. Now for it. Keep calm. Think of Melksham. Remember the drill."

Ken considered the fuse safe to remove, so called for a locking-ring key. This did not shift at once. He started to sweat a bit, as he tapped it gently with a hard wood timbering wedge. It yielded a bit. He was still safe. More taps, and it turned a bit more. Quarter-turn, half-turn, then a full circle. Ken got the ring clear. The fuse was free in its pocket – but on the lower side of the bomb. So, to stop it from sliding out he jammed a folded newspaper against the fuse-head, so that it would fall out with a little pressure. But not yet.

Ken paused. Half-way in his first bomb. The fuse should be safe. Now to withdraw it. He attached a length of builder's line to the discharger cap, still fixed to the fuse-head, and led this line through a spade handle as a fairlead. When all was set to his satisfaction he returned with the free end to a position where the corner of the house sheltered him from a direct view of the shaft of the bomb.

The sappers moved to their prearranged positions at opposite ends of the short tree-lined road; most of the houses had been evacuated, so Ken was left alone with his bomb. Only a bird kept him company, chirruping in a tree above.

A sudden hush seemed to fall, perhaps just because Ken had stopped work and became aware of the outside world again after those minutes in the shallow shaft. He pulled the slack line. It resisted. He noticed his heart beating. Another pull, and the line gave towards him, so that he lunged back a bit beside the wall of the house. The fuse must be out. Ken walked forward, peered down the hole, and saw the shiny fuse lying actually on the crumpled newspaper beside the bomb. He could do one – so there was no reason why he could not do them all. The worst was over. That was what he thought as he glanced round to take a last look at the tree-lined little road.

It was a year to the day after their engagement that Ken and Jo were married at Sleaford parish church on Saturday, 1 March 1941. Or as they were officially described: Muriel Joan Smith, elder daughter of Mr and Mrs A.J. Smith, and Lieutenant Kenneth C. Revis, of the Royal Engineers, only son of Mr and Mrs V.N. Revis, of Bedford.

Jo's father gave her away. As the two of them walked up the aisle, every one turned towards her. She was in a long powder-blue *moiré* taffeta dress topped by a lace headdress. In her arms bloomed a bouquet of red roses. Jo's small sister, Jane, was her bridesmaid. She was in darker blue velvet with matching cap, and swung a basket of cream roses. A little page boy in blue velvet trousers to match completed the scene. The only difference was Ken in his uniform.

The service followed its timeless pattern as the words of *Lead us, Heavenly Father, lead us,* and *Love Divine, all loves excelling,* wafted out on the early spring air. The vicar's voice and the couple's responses echoed around the church, yet even there they could not get away from the War, for an air-raid siren wailed out from its vantage-point on top of the Sessions House, just across the market-square. It did not interrupt the marriage, however, and in a few minutes the familiar *Wedding March* was accompanying them down the aisle towards an uncertain future. At present they could live only from day to day.

By a coincidence not apparent then, they chose Hove for a nine-day honeymoon, and it was in their room at the Dudley Hotel one morning that the phone rang. It was Karl Kenway from Haywards Heath, where Ken was due to report after his leave.

"I thought I'd tell you not to bother to come back here. You're posted to Preston Barracks, Brighton, on Monday. I'll send your stuff down to you by truck."

So, Ken only had to go a mile or two from Hove to reach his new base. Here he encountered his fresh section, including the wiry, grey-haired Sergeant Miller and the deep-tanned features of Lance-Sergeant Henley. At that stage, Ken knew nothing significant about Brighton and Hove.

The officers' mess made an amazing change from the willing but inexperienced efforts of the batman at Battle. Even though there was a war on, as Bomb Disposal knew too well, the niceties of an established barracks mess with its long-established customs were still observed.

One evening, soon after Ken's arrival, the officers had taken their places at the dining-table, after the O.C. troops had seated himself first. The senior mess waiter was in the act of filling a soup plate from a tureen standing on a hotplate on the serving-table, when the other waiter entered from the kitchen and gave him a whispered message. The senior waiter nodded, carried the plate of soup towards the head of the table, lowered it gently on to the mat before the O.C., tucked a napkin under his arm, and only then said quietly, "Good evening, sir. Excuse me, but the barracks are on fire. "A" Block, I believe, sir."

The O.C. rose and informed the other officers. They repeated the waiter's "Excuse me, sir" and scrambled from the dining-room. The steam from the soup rose into the air and evaporated as the dish lay untouched.

Ken nearly collided with a trailer pump party as he hurried down the mess steps and along the side of the parade square to the part of the block where his detachment was housed, thinking about the boxes of detonators kept in his office. But the blaze was nowhere near, and in less than half an hour came under control. They all resumed their places at the dining-table, and the senior mess waiter brought a fresh bowl of soup for the O.C.

Once settled in at Preston Barracks, Ken's life got into the erratic rhythm of Bomb Disposal: short spells of comparative quiet followed by bombs to be tackled, and no knowledge where or when the next one would fall or be reported. In fact, one of his first jobs from Brighton took him back along the South Coast towards Hastings, to Bexhill-on-Sea. The message reached him via the Regional Commissioner's Office, Group, and Company Headquarters. Ken took a squad to make a reccy and start to clear the danger. On his arrival, he found that the bomb had plunged into some allotments close to the railway line, disturbing a quantity of vital home-grown produce. A whole row of houses had already been evacuated by the local authorities, and rail traffic could only pass the point at slow speed in case the vibration from the normal rate set off the bomb.

"Danger: Unexploded Bomb" read the prominent police notice hung on a rope barrier stretched across the street. The constable posted to wait for Ken lowered the rope for the B.D. car and truck to pass over it. Then he accompanied Ken to the corner of an empty house, and as they both peered round it, rather like criminals, he pointed out the spot where the hole of entry could be seen, and then returned to his post at the barrier.

As far as Ken could tell by probing into the soft soil, the bomb had dived down, almost following the line of the railway track, and pierced the ground at a point about half the length of a cricket pitch from it.

Taking into account the size and direction of the hole and the nature of the ground, Ken marked out the ground above the position where he estimated the bomb to be lying, and the squad soon started excavation.

Normally they tried to dig vertically over the bomb, so that they came across it as near the centre of the shaft as possible. This did not always work out in practice, by any means, as the slightest variation in soil density could cause it to 'jink' aside in amazing ways. With sand, chalk, or abnormally waterlogged ground, for instance, bombs had been known to come to rest nose upward or even break the surface again. Ken met more than one case of this subsequently.

At the end of the first day on the Bexhill site, Ken realized that they would be hampered by water, so he arranged for the Auxiliary Fire Service to bring a trailer pump along each morning to empty the hole of the water that had gathered before his men started the day's digging. About six feet down, one of the sappers called up to Ken, who was engaged on the surface at the time, "Found something, sir."

This turned out to be the buckled tail of a 250-kg bomb, but beyond that depth it became quite impossible to tell which direction the rest of the weapon had taken, as the ground was so sodden. The next days followed a familiar pattern of plodding downward, timbering the shaft with the utmost difficulty, and scooping out filthy liquid mud by the hundreds of buckets full. At last, after a week or more of this depressing work, they reached a depth of twenty feet and the bomb itself. So, Ken's estimate of its position had been a good one; often a second shaft had to be sunk if a bomb could not be found, and sometimes a third and fourth!

Sinking the metal probe and stethoscope through the liquid mire, Ken ascertained that the bomb was not ticking. That always came as a slight relief. Next, to confirm the kind of bomb they had beneath them, Ken took off his overalls and battledress blouse, rolled his sleeves up to their highest extent, and plunged his hand and arm into the mud to feel for the shape of the bomb. The mud covered his arm almost to the shoulder before he could say for sure it was a 250-kg and find the fuse with his fingers. What proved impossible to do at that stage, of course, was to read the markings on the fuse.

This was an extremely awkward one to confront Ken so early in his B.D. days. As they scooped the mud, the bomb slowly sank deeper and deeper, and at the same time the mud steadily oozed through the timbering. A dilemma seemed to be reached, and it was bad enough having to handle bombs without making difficult decisions too. Ken realized they could not deepen the shaft to get nearer the bomb without lining it with waterproof material. This meant another delay. But the bomb seemed to be in the bed of an underground stream, and in danger of eluding them altogether if they spent much longer on it. He had to take account also of the restricted railway service and general inconvenience of an unexploded bomb.

Ken came to his decision. "I'm going to detonate it here," he told Sergeant Miller.

Working only by touch, with his arms still under the cold, clammy mud, he managed to get a guncotton charge wedged against the side of the bomb opposite the fuse-pocket. A length of underwater-burning safety-fuse led from it, projecting through the dark-brown liquid. In fact, all Ken could actually see was this thin fuse, the only visible link with what lay below him. They could only remove a small proportion of the timbering, but the mud and earth which sank into the shaft as a result would help to deflect the blast and destruction of the explosion away from the railway line, with its telegraph and signal wires.

Ken posted practically the whole squad to warn onlookers at various points of the impending explosion, and was just about to descend the shaft for the last time to light the fuse, when the policeman waved towards him from the end of the houses. Sergeant Miller, the only one still with him, went off to the corner and returned with the message that a woman in one of the near-by houses had just had a miscarriage.

Could Ken postpone the explosion until the ambulance fetched her? One more decision. Ken had already arranged for the Southern Railway to stop all trains along that section of the line, and the bomb was in imminent danger of sinking and dislodging the guncotton charge. So, Ken gave them three more minutes to get the woman away. He had to avoid failing to explode the bomb, or he might never have been able to recover or dispose of it.

The minutes passed. Then, leaving Sergeant Miller at the top of the shaft in case of any more last-second messages or miscarriages, Ken climbed down into the hole and lit the fuse. Smoke wisped from it, and the gunpowder thread hissed as he clambered up the muddy timbers, glad to be out of that hole at last. At ground-level again he joined Miller, and they walked away. Although a natural tendency would be to run for it, sappers never do this after lighting a detonating fuse, particularly when alone, since they might trip or fall on uneven ground and be unable to get clear of the explosion in time. With steady steps they reached the house and safety – and waited.

"It's taking a hell of a time, isn't it?" someone said, as they always did on similar occasions.

The ground suddenly shook. The sound struck their ears. Ken looked over the eaves of the building to see the sky darkened with erupted earth and jagged torn timber. This thudded all around the house, and then the lighter pieces pattered down over an interval of several seconds before quiet came again. The large blackened crater was still spitting pungent smoke when Ken approached, and as usual after a "blow" (as it was called) in wet ground, the surrounding soil looked surprisingly dry. Actually, it would be treacherously soft, like a quicksand. Ken examined the railway line and found no damage, so the trains were soon running regularly again as the little community around the allotments filtered back to their abandoned homes.

Back in Brighton, Ken and Jo had found a flatlet, where they were living only a stone's throw from the front. Literally a stone's throw, too, for late one evening a beach mine, detonated by a stray dog, hurled shingle from the beach that fell like hail on the road outside their first-floor window.

Jo had volunteered as an ambulance driver, and one night, as Ken fetched her from her tour of duty, the air-raid siren moaned out over the Regency town. As neither of them had to report for further duty then, they hurried home to bed, and about a quarter of an hour later several bombs burst nearby. Ken waited for the telephone in the hall to ring. The all-clear went first, then it did.

It was his duty corporal at the barracks reporting in routine way the various incidents. Then he added:

"Some of 'em didn't go off, sir."

Ken told the corporal to send the utility van to the flat to fetch him very early in the morning.

"Tell the police, will you, that I'll be making a reccy of U.X.B.s at the crack of dawn unless there's a high-category one among the bunch and I hear from them earlier."

Unexploded bombs were classified as high-category when they lay in a factory producing war materials, or else threatened other vital services or supplies. Otherwise, bombs had to be left for a minimum safe period to allow any time-delay to run out before attempting to tackle them.

First thing in the morning, with ozone strong on the air, Ken stepped into the van for his tour of U.X.B.s. One of the first he found which had not gone off lay at the bottom of the steps leading into an air-raid shelter. The inevitable policeman had roped the area off, and on Ken's arrival pointed towards the dark entrance of the shelter in the half-light. Ken spotted the bomb from the top of the steps – and went down them.

The bomb appeared to be in a sorry state. Almost cracked in half, it had sheared across near the fuse-pocket opening by its impact on the concrete canopy of the shelter. The bomb had holed this canopy in its flight, completely smashing part of it.

Closing in on the bomb, Ken found that this was going to be another sticky job. The fuse half-exposed; its head seriously abraded with the markings obliterated; the locking ring twisted and all but wrenched from its seating.

24

Ken decided that here was a case for drastic and immediate action. With the inside of the bomb dangerously damaged and exposed, anything might happen. Despite the danger, Ken had by this time gained considerable confidence, and so went back to the car for a hammer and cold chisel.

To the others in the car he said, "Keep clear till I tell you. It's in a bit of a mess. I'll have to split the fuse out by force."

Ken returned to the shelter, descended the steps, wedged a sandbag on each side of the shattered bomb to stop it rolling on the concrete floor, and began work. In a case like this, the first moment was the worst – and, occasionally, the last. Ken gripped his hammer and chisel with assurance, put the chisel in place, and hit it with the hammer.

No bang.

After that initial blow, he felt fairly confident that the trembler switch must have been damaged. He told himself so several times by way of comfort, but still avoided striking the delicate gaine end of the fuse, which he could actually see through the split fuse-pocket.

One hour later, with an aching back, yet warmed by the effort of muscle and mental power, he emerged into the full daylight with the damaged fuse and its gaine separated from the bomb and each other. He blinked at the sky. Behind him lay the 50-kg bomb case severed across like the two halves of an egg after cracking.

And talking of eggs, Ken had one for his breakfast in the mess, and felt he had earned it. That was not quite the end of this particular bomb story, for later in the day Ken was telephoned by the C.R.E. (Commander, Royal Engineers) and severely reprimanded for defusing a low-category bomb before waiting the requisite time. Ken had no chance to tell the Colonel the state of the bomb which prompted him to act accordingly, nor could he comment, of course, that it was highly dangerous to him, as well as Brighton. Still, Ken mused after he put down the receiver, it was just as well the Colonel did not know how he had done the job or he might have got into more serious hot water.

The emotions of a lifetime were being telescoped into these months, although Ken would eventually experience enough for several lives. As it was, by the time he received a posting to Horley, to command a two-section detachment there, he felt quite a veteran bomb-disposer.

Ken was certainly getting varied bombs to tackle, and the next strange case occurred almost as soon as he got to Horley. On the night of 26 October 1940, Captain Lord Claud Hamilton and his family, at Faygate, in Sussex, heard the swish and thump of two falling bombs, but no bangs afterwards. The following day a search in the grounds of the house revealed two small craters. At one of them, a young double-trunked beech-tree had been lifted bodily by the impact and thrown to one side. Both craters were concluded to be the result of small exploded bombs. Then, during the first half of 1941, no enemy raids disturbed that area. Nearly eight months later, on 11 July 1941, the Hamiltons heard a loud explosion in the grounds, and sent for Bomb Disposal.

Lord Claud Hamilton was then Comptroller and Treasurer to Queen Mary's household. As soon as Ken reached Faygate, he took the B.D. officer into the woods a little way from the mansion, and showed Ken a huge pit of a crater forty-five feet wide.

"Looks like a 500-kg bomb, sir," Ken suggested, as they examined a yard-thick tree that had been ripped out of the ground, roots and all, and the fresh yellow scars on the surrounding tree-trunks.

On their way back to the house for tea, Lord Hamilton explained to Ken about the sound of the two bombs the previous autumn. It seemed from the evidence that what they had heard were two large U.X.B.s and not small bombs which had gone off. Hamilton was naturally anxious for his family in view of one having self-detonated so long afterwards, and Ken promised to make a thorough search along the line which the enemy plane had come, using the definite evidence of the crater as a guide. Despite this he felt far from confident that he could find the entry hole of the other bomb, especially as the area was thickly wooded and a winter had come and gone since it fell. Luck plays its part in locating bombs, however, and Ken had a share of it after about an hour spent probing for some signs. He came across a small slanting aperture in the ground that might have been a rabbit-hole. It was almost hidden by leaves and twigs, but it attracted him unusually because of a broken branch lying across a tree root at the neck of the hole.

Ken took a chance on this, and launched digging operations. On the second day one of the sappers called to him, "You were right, sir, it's here."

There, sure enough, lay the battered tail-fins of a 500-kg bomb, suggesting that the rest of it would not be far away. The men went on digging, while Ken continued his probing.

With even apparently safe jobs, great care is essential in bomb disposal, so at Faygate they were all understandably apprehensive, since the gaping crater only 200 yards away had been caused by either the restarting of the clockwork delay mechanism in a fuse, or some slight vibration closing the trembler switch. Since their bomb was obviously from the same stick as the one that had gone off after all those months, exactly the same thing applied to it, and the most insignificant movement on the surface could spell a sudden end to all their lives.

No clock ticking. They were thankful for small mercies. When the shaft measured some sixteen feet down and the ground – not to mention the men – had become quite waterlogged, they suddenly stumbled on it. A 500-kg bomb lying on its side.

By now Ken had developed the inevitable fatalistic approach to his work, and felt more intrigue than fear. The water in the hole was stained and dark mustard in colour, while brighter yellow liquid trickled from the damaged fuse-head of the bomb. Ken assumed this to be partly dissolved picric acid, and took it that the inside of the fuse-pocket had suffered. He would have been more than human if the thought of the other bomb had not crossed his mind five yards down that shaft.

He ordered the squad to a safe position, and then grappled with the fuse, damaged and corroded. To get the fuse out, he had to make a lot of movement around the bomb. Several times it was struck quite severely, and the vibration echoed audibly within the shaft. Finally, the fuse was out.

He was still alive. B.D. was just that – a question of living from minute to minute, day to day. The mystery of the first explosion remained. Tentatively it was ascribed to a 17 clockwork fuse that had stopped and restarted again in the way which only clocks can. But since the bomb had gone off, no one could prove the presence of a clock, and in the absence of other evidence it was usual to presume that bombs in the same stick would be similarly fused. Whatever the answer, Ken survived his sojourn at Faygate, widening his range of experience at the same time.

One further sidelight on U.X.B. work around this period was the 'camouflet.' At Faygate and elsewhere, Ken always made his men work with lifelines around their waists in the early stages of each excavation, until it had really been established the bomb in question had not exploded underground. He had heard of cases where a squad had been called to a site where a normal hole of entry indicated the presence of an unexploded bomb. Yet, in fact, the bomb had exploded beneath the ground entirely and because of the hardness of the subsoil or rock, it had failed to lift out the huge cone of ground to form the familiar crater.

These chambers caused by subterranean explosions were called 'camouflets,' and constituted a constant menace. If a sapper broke through the crust of earth between the chamber and the surface he might plunge into the cavity and be poisoned by carbon monoxide gas trapped there from the explosion. One good breath was fatal. Tragedies like this did actually happen, though Ken never experienced one with any of his men.

27

Soon after being moved to Horley, Ken and Jo went to live with a Charles Buxton and his daughter, Paddy, and it was their house which formed the setting for Jo's twenty-first birthday party. The house had a dining-room with an unusual minstrel gallery, while the French windows were flung open to a perfect brick terrace. This led in turn to a rocky pool fed by water tumbling down from a cairn. And Ken and Jo and all their friends danced the whole warm August night away. A fragment of time torn out of war.

Another unreal day in that happy summer at Horley was the London wedding of John Price, with a sumptuous reception at a large London hotel. Ken met some of his O.C.T.U. friends again.

Perhaps the precious quality of those days was their very transience. If so, this applied especially to Bomb Disposal, whose losses still steadily grew. One of the special friends of Ken and John Price, who attended that wedding, did not live much longer. That was the way it went. *C'est la guerre.*

Meanwhile, Ken and Jo were being shifted around regularly. From Horley to Ripon, in Yorkshire, for a refresher course, and to take minds off actual operations for a while. The course was no sinecure, though, for all the while there were fresh facts and techniques to be mastered. And from Ripon to Hollingbourne and Wrotham successively. There the bomb-disposal war went on as usual, but the memorable things to Ken about the two places did not concern the enemy at all.

The minute officers' mess at Hollingbourne consisted of a tiny cottage, in which Ken and the one other officer lighted their way up the narrow stairs to bed with an oil lamp. The house at Wrotham turned out to be less primitive, but provoked a question never answered to this day. Who had occupied the place before the Army moved in? Because on the door of Ken's bedroom, painted in pure gold-leaf, was the name "Bluebell"!

Then back to Surrey, to Send, near Guildford. Two B.D. sections occupied Heath House there, and Ken and Jo went to live with Robin Young and her seven-year-old son Christopher, whose home was only three minutes' walk from the detachment headquarters, or H.Q. Her husband had been killed earlier in the War during an air raid on Ford aerodrome, where he was stationed in the Fleet Air Arm. She turned Pembroke House and its outbuildings and paddock into a war-time smallholding.

Eventually Robin and Jo, who combined so well, were managing a cow, eighty rabbits more or less, geese, ducks, chickens, a sty of pigs, and half a dozen goats for good measure. Hawk, a massive billy-goat, acted so aggressively that Ken had to help drag him by a

28

thick chain into the pen each evening. Robin's house at Send would have still greater significance the following year, but meanwhile it was the spring of '42, and Ken received a return posting to Preston Barracks.

As if in the form of light relief before the days to come, one of Ken's first missions back at Brighton was to a rather remarkable bomb. It started in a normal enough way as a telephone-call from company H.Q.

"U.X.B. in Seaford," followed by the bare details.

Still early in the morning, Ken and his squad sped the ten miles or so eastward to Seaford, where a police-officer led them to a pub called The Plough.

"There it is, sir. Well, if that's all, I'll be saying good morning." And with that he had marched off in the opposite direction. Ken moved nearer to the spot and saw a 250-kg bomb lying on the floor of an outside lavatory beside the inn. The door had been pushed fully open, and the porcelain basin cracked in a couple of places. The fuse was even conveniently on top of the bomb. It could scarcely have been in a better position from Ken's point of view, and as a B.D. job it proved reasonably uneventful. He carried out his drill, and when he got to the stage of withdrawing the fuse, he crouched down beside the wall of The Plough and tugged on his length of string. The fuse came out. The job was done.

But the amazing thing about the bomb Ken learned later when the police-officer returned to check that all had gone well.

"Shall I show you how it got there, sir?" he asked Ken.

The 250-kg bomb had hit the road first of all, scooped a big bit out of it some twelve to eighteen inches deep, and ricocheted on its way. From the road it dived through the wall of a garage eight feet high, and ploughed a way clean through two cars parked bonnet to bonnet – pausing only to leave its tail-fins neatly reposing on the back seat of one. Then the bomb really got going again. It leapt on through the far wall of the garage and across a graveyard, chipping several headstones as it went, and burst through a schoolroom wall. Careering over the desks, it pierced the opposite wall of the form-room and reached the side of the inn. By now it was tiring, and it could do no more than scud across the surface into the toilet.

As someone said afterwards, "It must have wanted to get there badly!"

This fantastic course resulted presumably from the first ricochet on the road, when it took on virtually a horizontal direction, with all the force of its fall still behind it. The detective work went one step farther: another bomb in the same stick exploded and stopped the church clock at 4.55 that morning – a couple of hours before Ken's arrival – so that must have been the exact time they were dropped.

There was nothing like being in Bomb Disposal for making fresh friends in an unconventional way. George Cook lived with his wife at Patcham, and Ken met them because a 1,000-kg bomb tore its way into the flower bed outside their French windows one night early in May 1942. Luckily it lay unexploded – only a yard or two from the foundations of their home.

Ken and his sappers dug down and reached the large bomb comparatively quickly, as it had been dropped during a low-level attack over the coast, and therefore had not penetrated more than a dozen feet into the chalky ground of the garden – a less adventurous course than the Seaford bomb a quarter its size.

After checking for any clock ticking, Ken discharged it electrically in the usual way, and on the fourth day there extracted the fuse, as he had now done dozens of times. In fact, he was almost blasé about bomb disposal. After they left the Cooks' garden with the bomb safely on the B.D. lorry, Ken and his men experienced a gesture that reminded them what these bombs actually meant in terms of people's lives and homes saved.

Many Patcham people had to be evacuated for a few days while the bomb was being handled, and Ken received many inquiries each day until the job ended. Then they asked him to take his squad to a special thanksgiving service on the following Sunday. On that day, the little local church was packed with people sitting not only in the pews, but on backs of pews and on the floor. They even stood in the churchyard outside, thronging at the opened windows while Ken and his little group arrived. Wearing their best battledress, the B.D. section were shown to the front pew of the crowded church, where they sat in some embarrassment.

As the sun slanted in on that fine May morning, Ken read the lesson.

As mementoes of the bomb and its removal, Sergeant Woodrow, who worked with Ken, received an engraved silver cigarette-case and each of the men an engraved silver identity-disc. Ken himself was handed a silver cup engraved as follows:

PRESENTED TO LIEUT. K.C. REVIS, R.E.
12TH BOMB DISPOSAL COY, R.E.
IN APPRECIATION OF COURAGE AND SKILL
SHOWN IN DEFUSING 1000KG
PATCHAM, 13.5.42.

Ken realized why the inscription did not add "enemy bomb" after the size. George Cook came up to him, he recalled, and asked him casually, "What do you chaps call these bombs?"

Ken answered, "1000 kg" So, the engraver had obviously taken this at its face value. Naturally the cup became one of Ken's favourite possessions, for it gave a tangible sign that their work was appreciated by the civilian population.

And Ken, for his part, frequently saw what people had to endure from enemy raids. Once he went in a house where a U.X.B. had pierced the roof and the kitchen ceiling, and lodged in the gas oven. He noticed, as well, the beds upstairs, obviously left in an instant of terror as the bomb crashed through the rear of the building. The family had rushed out of the house in the darkness of the previous night – and here was all the evidence of that moment.

Ken seemed to be meeting every aspect of the unexpected, which was always a feature of B.D. work. For just at this time, too, he was due to detonate a bomb that had turned out to be awkward to tackle any other way – when a dog sauntered on to the scene.

Ken lit the fuse beside the bomb, returned from the shaft, and reached cover to wait for the bang. The thin wisp of smoke or smell of the powder burning must have attracted the animal, for it suddenly seemed to appear and look down the shaft. Ken watched it for a moment, his head outside cover. He could not bear the thought of the dog getting killed, but no one could rescue him as there were only seconds left before the bomb would explode.

Ken yelled and waved his arms at him, but he took no notice at all. Ten seconds to go now, and the animal was still standing and then wandering four or five feet from the side of the shaft. Ken was still shouting to him when the bomb burst. Unprotected by cover, Ken watched for a moment as the dog was bowled over and over like a leaf toppled in the wind. Then he had to get his head down quickly as the debris peppered all around. As soon as it had settled, Ken looked up again anxiously towards the hole, and there, as large as life, was the dog racing away from the spot – safe.

Chapter 3

BOMB UNDER A CHURCH

So, to the Southwick bomb, one of the most complex B.D. jobs of all. Lieutenant Karl Kenway was needed in another area, so Ken took over the bomb from him, and it turned out to be quite a legacy. The original reccy reported that a 1000-kg bomb – the one-ton equivalent – had dived into the graveyard of a church at Southwick, near Brighton, and was believed to be lying very deep under the building. Before Ken came into the picture, two shafts reaching down to forty feet each had been hacked out of the ground without the semblance of a trace of the bomb or its tail. The side pressure on a deep shaft is considerable enough without a building on the ground. In this case the church tower would exert a dangerously heavy strain on one side, so the whole tower had been taken down faithfully stone by stone, each being numbered and methodically stacked for rebuilding after the war.

When Ken and Karl heard about the take-over Karl said, "You'd better come out and have a look at the job yourself before I push off." Although it was already dark, they set off by car to Southwick, and after a drink at the pub they went on to the site itself. Ken peered through the gloom as his companion pointed in the direction of a third shaft, which had recently been started. Kenway saw that the first two shafts were carefully filled in with sandbags – no mean job in itself. This always had to be done scrupulously, to guard against the chance of their falling in and causing casualties or other damage. Often, too, fresh shafts were sunk near the earlier ones, and unless these were properly filled, timbering for correct support could not be done.

Ken felt quite shaken by the first surprising sight of the job. The church looked like a toy snapped in two by a destructive child; timber and broken tombstones lay scattered about everywhere; the stack of masonry blocks stood grey and neglected; and in the lane near the church wall rose a mound of earth and chalk as tall as a train.

Before he could see it, Ken said, "You've got a pump working, then?"

"Yes – a dewatering set. It's so close to the sea here we've got to have it running day and night to try and keep the subsoil as dry as we can."

This complicated outfit consisted first of a large diesel-engine-driven pump mounted on a four-wheel trailer. From this ran a twelve-inch header pipe, lying in a very shallow trench on the surface of the churchyard and completely surrounding the whole shaft area with a rectangular pipe system. At intervals along this main pipe, smaller steel pipes were connected to it by flexible couplings, and driven down between thirty and forty feet into the ground. These subsidiary pipes sucked up the hundreds of gallons of subsoil water, which were carried through the header pipe to the pump. The pipes had cutting edges at the bottom, and grille holes to allow for this passage of the water. Once back to the pump, a twelve-inch pipe discharged it at full hose pressure, and as they were burrowing in bowels of white chalk this pipe looked as if it were 'delivering the milk' – for the foot-thick stream of liquid continuously forced out of it was pure milky white.

They had been working on the job for several weeks already, and now attention focused on the excavation in the centre. Not only did the dewatering set chug away every night, but a working party actually slept there, too, under a tarpaulin shelter. They had organized their own night cooking arrangements, and mattresses lay on wooden boards in the shelter. In addition to these on-the-spot facilities, the section as a whole lived in a little house down the road a short way. So, the set was in full flood at 10 p.m. on the night Ken formally received command of the Southwick incident.

So that was that. Ken took over as the third shaft had groped down fifteen feet. Still some twenty-five feet to go to reach the estimated depth of the bomb. As no one ever knows the exact state of a bomb buried in the ground without having exploded, already the chance existed that the suction-pipes operating at nearly that depth might very easily disturb it fractionally and set off a trembler fuse or clock. This danger was present through days and then weeks of digging. Later other dangers would make it seem slight.

Ken grew accustomed to the steady sound as the powerful pump throbbed away week after week, and the shaft went down to 20, 25, 30, 35 feet. The night shift took over regularly in the evening, and they even replenished the oil in the sump of the diesel motor without stopping it. In fact, the throbbing became so much a part of the job and their daily lives that – like factory workers – they soon took it for granted and in the end hardly noticed it at all.

Till one day, quite unexpectedly, the pump faltered with a strangled sort of note, slowed down, and finally stopped dead. The silence seemed really uncanny as the party looked at each other for a moment. The jet of milky water soon lost its pressure, fell to a trickle, and then followed suit and stopped.

If the delay were too long all their weeks of work might be wasted. After a two-second stupor by everyone there, the lance-sergeant in charge of the dewatering set rushed over to it, lifted up the bonnet, and started to examine it. He unscrewed the fuel-pipe and found it had fractured.

Ken was on the spot by now, and grabbed it out of his hand, realizing the urgency of the situation. Luckily, Ken had happened to train a civilian emergency bomb-disposal team at the near-by Shoreham gasworks, and he thought that they would help him if they could. Putting his foot down hard on the accelerator of the Army car, he headed for that ugly group of gaswork buildings by the sea at Shoreham, and drove straight inside.

It did not take long to explain the situation to them, as he retrieved the fuel-pipe out of the back of the car, and they put the repair through as a rush job in under an hour.

With a hasty word of thanks, Ken put the pipe on the back seat again and tore back by car to the bomb site. He and the lance-sergeant screwed the repaired fuel-pipe back into position and started up. The engine fired again, picked up to its normal familiar note, and water began to gush out of the delivery end once more after a total stoppage of just under two hours. It was just as well the job had not taken twice or three times as long, for even in that brief time nearly fifteen feet of water had completely flooded the lower half of the shaft.

The next problem was to suck out these thousands of gallons swishing about and swamping the precious shaft, but this had to be done slowly and with infinite care, or the sides of the excavation might be sucked in and collapse. The timbering all the way down was stout 4-by-4 inch, but the pressures built up on the sides of a shaft forty feet deep are high. Nevertheless, the milky pool slowly subsided as they put a fresh suction-pump on it, and the last few feet of the shaft could then be sunk.

The same thing very nearly happened again one day soon afterwards, just before reaching the required depth, but the fault this time was found almost before the diesel had time to stop, and no harm was done. Then came the next day and the bottom of the shaft. Forty feet down under a Southwick churchyard, all dug by hand in the worst

34

possible conditions. Winter was coming on now properly, too, and the coastal site could scarcely be more exposed.

The next nasty stage was to start cutting out a four-foot-square tunnel horizontally from the bottom of the main shaft, in the general direction the bomb was thought to have fallen. Their chances of locating it did not seem too good even with the shaft safely sunk, as they had no real scrap of evidence yet as to its precise position. The tunnel would need to be some twenty feet long to tell if the bomb were in that direction. So, they started and progressed slowly, in the manner of prisoner-of-war escape tunnels, where every ounce of soil had to be disposed of before they could continue. And with the weight of forty feet of ground on top of it, the tunnel had to be supported even more than the main upright shaft with timbering. All this took time, and a week or so passed before they reached fifteen feet along.

Then Ken was resting on a bucket for removing chalk from the bottom of the shaft one morning, probing between the boards into the sides of the shaft, when, entirely by chance, he pulled out a scrap of aluminium not three inches long.

"I've found it," he cried out to the rest of the party dispersed above him and in the tunnel he had recently left.

This was not exactly accurate, for it did not prove to be the bomb itself, but a strip of the type of metal used for the cast tail-fins of 1,000- kg German bombs.

"Hey – you can stop work on the tunnel!"

Ken decided this at once because the aluminium was on another side of the shaft from where they were digging the tunnel! Then he ordered the tunnel to be thoroughly plugged with sandbags and earth, and a fresh one to be launched from the side where his only clue had come to light.

So, they started the second tunnel – at the bottom of the third shaft! Inch by inch it grew, with Ken taking his turn at the face of it with a miner's pick and shovel. They got light from electric bulbs run off car batteries on the surface. The new tunnel actually ran at about ninety degrees to the previous one, still horizontal to the bottom of the shaft, of course. Two days later again, they were four feet along the tunnel when another wonderful clue seemed sent from heaven. The first one was not really conclusive, but no one could argue about this: plumb in the centre of the line of burrowing, a 15-inch jagged tail-fin lying in the chalky subsoil. Taking into account the time spent by Karl Kenway before Ken's time, they had devoted several months to this bomb, yet here for the first time lay a concrete sign of its presence. And at least it had dropped as deep as they were.

Now that they were probably near the bomb, they proceeded with care, as all the time, too, there existed the double danger of the tunnel collapsing as well as the bomb going off. Either would be fatal. As the tunnel slowly inched forward, Ken kept check on everything, his surveying experience coming in useful for problems of stresses and similar points. They were nearly underneath the church tower now, taken down not only for its weight's sake but because of slight cracks, too.

When above ground Ken used to go into the deserted church each day to examine the cracks in the floor and walls of its tower-base, to see if their operations were causing any more movement. The cracks could not really be considered surprising, since a one-ton bomb travelling at hundreds of miles an hour had threshed through forty feet of close-packed earth and chalk only a few feet from the flint and stone church.

During the next week, as throughout the operation, every so often the bucket would be brought up from the base of the shaft. But instead of soil and other excavation from the tunnel, there would be a skull sitting there grinning up at them. Sometimes one of the sappers would have added parted hair and a moustache to it to make it a bit more gruesome! The bomb ripped open a number of graves in its passage, and their digging disturbed more of them, so Ken had the job of reinterring these skulls and other human remains, which came up with alarming regularity.

On the tenth day of digging the second tunnel, they had reached some sixteen to eighteen feet. Ken had been working with the chaps at the face of it most of that morning, cramped in a crouched position, with the floor of the tunnel always awash. The light from their bulbs danced on the walls and roof, glistening white, as they took turns with pick and shovel at the four-foot-square face. Ten days of this after the futility of the first tunnel had reduced their spirits a little, as Ken made his way up to the surface at midday. He wondered how many times he had climbed up that shaft already.

He was back by a gas fire in the little semi-detached house, munching a cookhouse pie, when Sergeant Woodrow literally lunged into the room, breathlessly excited.

"We've found it, sir!"

Ken never did finish that pie. Instead, the two of them trotted along the 150 yards between the house and the site, with Woodrow telling him about it as they went.

Elated, Ken jumped over the churchyard wall, picked his way over the uneven ground, and scrambled down the ladder – almost slipping several rungs in his haste. Then he ducked along the tunnel to where

36

a small group of smiling sappers greeted him, pointing eagerly. Ken looked and saw the circular shape of a large tail-end filler plug just protruding through the roof of the tunnel right above his head. If they had bored only a foot deeper, they would have missed the bomb altogether. So now they were six yards along a tunnel forty feet below the surface – with a one-ton bomb right on top of them. To some people, this situation must have resembled a nightmare, but B.D. were used to practically anything by now: nearly Christmas, 1942.

"It's a 1,000-kg all right," Ken confirmed. And what they saw meant something more. The tail end was pointing straight down, so the nose of the bomb must be vertically upward. It had apparently reversed its downward-pointing direction on entering the chalky ground, and come to a stop the other way up. This in turn meant that the weight of the thing – fully one ton – must be concentrated downward in as narrow a width as possible, hence the strain of supporting it could not be worse. They would clearly encounter some difficulties before it could be lowered into the small space of the tunnel below to reveal a sight of its fuse. For that was still the all-important part of it.

Remembering his strict sequence of drill, Ken got a stethoscope on this only portion yet exposed, and listened.

"Not a sound," he said, "but we've still got to be careful. Don't forget, chaps."

One of them jammed a stout piece of timber under the bomb, and then worked away round it with a pick, while Ken crouched in the corner scanning the roof for the slightest movement. The bomb was wedged tightly, but a ton on top of them could not be ignored. While they remained at the face, there was no room for any of the others, so Ken and the sapper took turns with the pick. Working in this highly restricted and uncomfortable way, they enlarged the chamber at the end of the tunnel until a third of the bulk of the bomb hung exposed overhead, like some strange stalactite curving out of the domed roof. It gave the impression of being supported entirely on the original length of timber propped under it, but, in fact, the ground above it still clamped it sufficiently to stop it falling.

As they picked away at the chalk, water seeped in all the time from the sides and the roof, swilling the slopping floor of the tunnel. If the pump were to fail now, they would have to get out quickly, as the tunnel would fill in a few minutes. Just one more thought in case they relaxed too much. On and on they picked their way till half the bomb hung above them. Then Ken thought it was time to stop.

All this took time, of course, and the next phase was to construct a crib of short timbers to within a fraction of an inch or so of the tail-plug of the bomb. They hoped that when the weapon did in fact show signs of release from the roof, the crib would take its weight and control its slide towards the tunnel. Here once more Ken's pre-war work helped as he made complicated calculations of the stresses likely when the 1,000-kg bomb became free.

Eventually they prepared the crib and put the final touches to it. Then Ken got one of the sappers to go on picking away around the bomb until he estimated that the original timber strut was taking virtually the complete load of the bomb. Using a small sledgehammer with some degree of delicacy, Ken next tapped the bottom end of the supporting timber. With the help of the sapper and an assortment of levers, Ken gradually got the end of the timber strut to move a little. The bomb began to stir. More sledgehammering and levering, and the timber strut slipped out, accompanied by creaks and groans from the crib as the filler plug bit into the top timber by the bomb's own weight. Then suddenly the strut was out and the bomb cradled safely above them – still only half of it visible, though.

They had to be absolutely sure that any unnecessary movement was avoided, in case the bomb went off. They also had to make certain it did not drop and crush or injure anyone. So, the answer involved wedging it securely at each side on to a sloping ramp built into the tunnel. As the bomb slid out of its nest, they moved the wedges down one position at a time, so that at every stage it was fully wedged against the sides.

When they had at last coaxed it nearly down to floor-level, still creaking away in protest as it fell, they could begin to turn its course towards the face of the tunnel. By this method of wedging and releasing it from either flank they got its entire ton weight lying on the slippery wet floor of the tunnel, its wooden ramp below water-level.

At this point, the bomb blocked the tunnel completely, and their sole light came from the bulbs, so that a sense of claustrophobia swept over them until they busied themselves on the next job.

Before beginning this, however, Ken naturally craned his neck round to peer up into the chamber vacated by the bomb. He saw something surprisingly beautiful that imprinted itself in his memory. Above was the perfectly smooth shape carved out by the nose of the bomb: a white arched dome with flints flashing and glistening like gems in the floodlight. For a minute he forgot where he was, in the strangeness of the scene. But then the problems still ahead attracted his attention. The roof and walls of that chamber at the end of the tunnel were completely unsupported by timbers and quite likely to cave in at any time, so he did not want to lose a moment.

With the bomb blocking the tunnel, they rolled it on its ramp for Ken to get a look at the fuse for the first time. He found a 15 fuse with the fuse-head damaged: scored and marked where it had hit hard rock met when diving on its U-shaped course through the ground.

The 15 fuse should have been reasonably safe to withdraw after going through the drill of discharging electricity, but the additional hazard lately had been anti-handling devices – or booby-traps.

When the Germans discovered that Bomb Disposal were learning their various fuse-head markings and could withdraw some of their fuses they started to supply the Luftwaffe with bombs containing fuses that looked harmless enough but sometimes concealed a booby-trap. This could explode the bomb quite independently of the main fuse if anyone tried to pull it out of the fuse-pocket even a fraction of an inch. Naturally the ZUSS 40, as the deadly device was called, carried no warning marking on the outside of the fuse, and risks were often inevitable where the fuse-head had been damaged.

Ken discharged its electricity with the cap and at last came to the fuse itself. Both the fuse-head and locking ring had been damaged, and the fuse-key would not fit, so it looked like being a case of hammer and chisel – never the best tools to have to use on an unexploded bomb. Ken had literally to hack the locking ring away. Its metal was badly burred, and so the clank of his hammer on the head of the chisel echoed out of the tunnel. The chisel bit into the ring, and slowly Ken turned it round – by the 'brute-force method' not found in the drill book, but resorted to by most Bomb Disposal officers at one time or another.

With the locking ring at last clear, and Ken still alive, he prepared to extract the fuse itself by the rather crude but effective 'length-of-string' system. With the string securely attached, he crawled out of the eighteen feet of tunnel and unwound it the forty feet of the shaft as he climbed the ladder. A few more feet took him to the far side of the church wall, where their lorries stood parked. Although this was considered a safe remote-control way of withdrawing a fuse, Ken had to admit to himself that if the bomb did conceal a Zuss 40, a ton of high explosive erupting so near would still probably have killed some of them.

He jerked the string. No bang. So no booby-trap.

The end was finally in sight now. They managed to draw the bomb along the tunnel to the bottom of the shaft and then up to ground-level by winch and steel cable. A further drag across the bumpy churchyard, up a ramp into a waiting lorry, and they were headed home for Preston Barracks with their load. All of them were still smeared from hair to feet with chalk, mud, and grime, but felt triumphant and elated. And by a supreme stroke of fortune, the night was New Year's Eve, 1942-43. Ken celebrated the end of the 1,000-kg with the end of another year.

Next morning, New Year's Day, Ken and a couple of sappers set about splitting out the crystalline high explosive from the defused bomb with a long crowbar and a sledgehammer. While they did this on the parade square, they noticed that everyone who came near and saw them attacking the bomb in this way vanished from the vicinity in a flash!

So ended the episode of the Southwick bomb. Many people thought that Ken deserved the George Cross for it.

Chapter 4

CLEARING THE BEACHES

In the spring Ken was sent to Ripon, in Yorkshire, on a refresher course at the School of Military Engineering. This gave him one of those periodical changes so essential to Bomb Disposal personnel, and he found himself throwing grenades and anti-tank bombs, firing spigot mortars, and generally getting up to date in conventional Army warfare.

Then, when the course was nearly over, he came down to breakfast one morning in the large dining-room at Harper Barracks, where a handful of officers in battledress stared over their coffee-cups at newspapers propped on wooden stands. As an Auxiliary Territorial Service, or A.T.S., waitress brought Ken his porridge, a voice behind him said, "Morning, old boy."

Karl Kenway pulled up a chair and sat down beside him. Ken had now known him on and off for nearly two and a half years, ever since their meeting as brother subalterns when Ken had been posted to Haywards Heath fresh from O.C.T.U. in January 1941. And more recently, of course, Ken took over that Southwick bomb from him, so they had a lot in common: the bond of shared experience.

As Ken sugared his porridge, Kenway slit open a letter he had brought in from the rack in the hall, and started to read it. After a few seconds he said excitedly, "We're on mines, Ken. This is from French, and he's heard from Group that some of the sections are being put on to mine clearance."

So now it was the beaches for them both. They had been half expecting the news for some time, but it still came as a surprise. They seemed to have been on U.X.B.s so long that nothing would move them except the end of the War. And not knowing what their future held, or how this change might influence it, they talked together over porridge and the rest of breakfast before setting out for the exercises that day.

Ken had not thought much about beach mines before, but he did so now. He knew, of course, that millions of these small anti-invasion, anti-personnel mines had been sown under the beaches of Britain, and now lay dormant. With the danger of German invasion past, and the need for beaches to rehearse the Allies' own invasion then being planned, a start had to be made clearing the shores. The losses to B.D. men would prove just as tragic as their operations against enemy bombs, but all that as yet remained ahead.

The Ripon refresher course broke up early the following week, and Ken was quickly on the train travelling south to Haywards Heath again. This time Ken arrived at detachment headquarters as a seasoned officer with a brilliant record of bomb-disposal behind him. He reported by telephone to his company commander, Major "Dutchy" Holland, at Horsham, who told Ken that they would drive down next day to Bracklesham Bay, West Sussex, where Ken's new section was already assembled and active.

Midsummer, mid-morning, and already hot when Ken's car pulled up behind the O.C.s own vehicle outside Caffyn's, the large garage that was No. 12 Company headquarters in Horsham. Major Holland was already in his car, and did not notice Ken's arrival or salute, for he was sprawled over the back of the front seats trying to arrange three short Polish mine-detectors on the floor. After he squeezed backward out of the car, he greeted Ken, and then added: "Be careful with your kit on those detectors – they're new." Dutchy clearly took his job seriously, which was just as well when faulty gear could be disastrous.

These marked Ken's first introduction to the latest specialized detecting equipment for beach mines. He was familiar with normal long-handled Polish mine-detectors from his Aldershot training on the O.C.T.U. course, but these short-handled ones were new to him – enabling a man crawling forward to sweep the ground or beach in front of him while holding the detector in one hand and supporting himself on the other.

With Holland at the wheel, they were soon speeding towards the coast, the sun scorching down on the signal-red-painted mudguards distinguishing a Bomb Disposal vehicle; and on the top of the bonnet, a vivid yellow patch of gas-detector paint.

Dutchy covered the twenty-odd miles to Worthing in well under the hour, and then branched westward to Littlehampton. Even in war, this coastal strip of Sussex seemed pretty peaceful as the car hummed past the old church at Goring-by-Sea, the neat little bungalows at Ferring, and the quaint village of Rustington.

A section was already at work on the beach at Littlehampton, and as Dutchy drew up a little way from the shore, the burly frame of Lance-Sergeant Henley came over to the car. His section commander and sergeant were both out of hailing distance along the shore at the time, so he reported progress to the O.C. Ken greeted him as well, as they had been together many times on bombs in the past. Now this new job marked a fresh phase in the War. Ken liked Henley very much, and remembered his ruddy face always seemed ready to smile; actually, in his mind, Ken thought of him as looking very much like the film-actor Richard Dix.

Henley was to be killed that same autumn.

After a last exchange of information, Dutchy drove on, and after lunch the car reached the narrow twisting lanes leading to the coast at Bracklesham Bay, where Lieutenant Francis Drew had been in temporary command of Ken's section. Before the war, the part of Bracklesham Bay concerning them had been fringed by a collection of wooden bungalows and chalets, but although these still stood there they were deserted and neglected behind the bank of shingle. Ken saw rows of grey concrete anti-invasion blocks stretched all along the shore, interlaced with barbed wire. The torn, flapping roofing felt of the buildings and the tufts of coarse beach-grass added to the blocks and barbed wire to present a desolate scene, even on a summer's day.

The section had pitched camp several days earlier, and Ken was to share a tent with Lieutenant John "Ginger" Warren, his opposite number in charge of the other section of their detachment. Major Holland took Drew back to Horsham with him that afternoon, and Ken was all set for his new assignment: the battle against beach mines.

Most of the mines lying beneath the beaches were Naval B type and weighed just over fifty pounds each. The drill for detecting and dealing with them was quite complicated but efficient, as Ken soon discovered.

First of all, an Non-Commissioned Officer, or N.C.O., swept a particular path, using the familiar Polish mine-detector. This consisted of a large, flat dish-shaped search-coil at the end of a bamboo handle held by the operator. On his back was slung an amplifying set, connected to a pair of headphones over his ears. As he swept, variation in the sound pitch reaching his headphones from the search-coil disclosed the presence of ferrous metals such as iron or steel. Tuning controls on the handle of the detector helped identify the exact spot.

Behind the N.C.O. followed a sapper whose job was to mark the spot indicated while the first man held the search head motionless. Their method of doing this was with a light red wooden marker for each mine located, at the same time showing the path so far swept with a white marking-tape.

Where the danger of a detonation existed – which was almost always – Ken had to separate his men in order to reduce the risk of casualties. So only when the first pair had advanced far enough so as not to cause injury to anyone else if they set off a mine could Ken allow the section sergeant or lance-sergeant to follow and expose the mine itself with a trowel or shovel. The arming handle of the mine was normally 'in,' making the weapon active, and the N.C.O. who exposed the mine then had to pull out the arming handle with a special forked tool.

Then the same safety distance had to be allowed again before Ken, as section officer, brought up the rear and removed the lid, extracted the fuse, and dismantled the mine altogether. Working in this way, they were able to use more than one team creeping forward at respectable distances from each other.

In practice, however, the drill did not always work, because the arming handle had frequently rusted. On many occasions subsequently they had to lift out mines in this rather critical condition for detonation elsewhere. Or where the explosion could not set off or bury other beach mines, they blew them up where they lay. But chain reaction was a dangerous hazard that could never be overlooked.

Ken got off to a grim start. During his very first morning on the beach, Ken had started detecting with his team when he noticed a brown-stained crater like a small shell-hole a little way off. He inquired what it was.

They told him that it was where Sapper Edwards had been blown to pieces a few days previously.

One of the particular problems on this stretch of beach at Bracklesham was the coarse grass growing through the shingle, since this prevented them lowering the head of their detector near enough to the beach to pick up a sufficiently audible signal in the headphones. Ken saw the danger of this situation, and decided it would be better to burn the grass to get down to the shingle itself. There was bound to be some risk even in this procedure, but it seemed to be the lesser of two evils.

No special gear existed yet to cope with such a necessity, so they had to improvise. They found the remains of some kapok floats, and twisted wire handles around large chunks of this material. Soaking these in petrol, they ignited them and flung them rapidly into the grass-choked minefield. It did the trick on the whole, although detection and dismantling after such a process naturally became a grimy business. They had their reward at the end of those summer days, however, with a swim in the cool evening sea.

Casualties were caused all too often by momentary lapses on the beaches, and it was to try to avoid mental fatigue or strain that sweeping spells were limited to about an hour at a time. Despite this, there was always the occasional incident.

One mid-morning at Bracklesham, with the sun searing down, the section was enjoying its break after the first session that day. The men were sitting around at the side of a stretch of the minefield as one of them brought the 'dixie' of tea into the group. He poured it into the raised mugs, and someone handed Ken his drink. They were all there except Corporal Murphy, still on his way in from a farther section. Ken relaxed with his mug of tea and sat watching the water breaking softly. A good moment in the morning.

Suddenly he turned his head and saw Murphy a mere ten yards away, walking towards them for his mug of tea.

In a flash Ken knew what had happened.

"For Heaven's sake, stand still – we haven't swept there."

The short, sleek-haired Cockney stopped dead, one foot in front of the other, swaying slightly. He had mistaken the white tapes marking an old minefield for a swept section.

Ken got up quickly, snatched up a Polish detector, put on a pair of headphones, adjusted the pitch on them, and then found a piece of metal to test it out. The detector worked, and he was ready. Sweeping into the field in arcs towards Murphy, Ken found mine after mine on the route. Another sapper following up marked the mines, as they made several detours before reaching the corporal, although only a dozen paces away from the tea-party. The other sapper taped their path at the same time, so that the three of them could then reverse and tread back safely through the minefield. Ken's tea was still warm enough to drink when they got back and sat down again.

"Thanks, sir," said Murphy.

The rest of the day and, in fact, the whole Bracklesham Bay sweep went off without further incident, and Ken next received orders to move eastward to the other extreme end of the country's coastline. His assignment: to sweep the beach stretching east from Newhaven Harbour as far as Seaford. So, Ken struck camp and their convoy set out: a dispatch rider, his personal utility van, 15-cwt truck, and three large lorries. They threaded a way past now-familiar towns – Worthing, Shoreham, Southwick, Brighton.

Enormous columns of a gyn-tackle towering high into the sky, a glaring orange in the afternoon sun, heralded the approach to Newhaven. With these gyn lags, quite large vessels could be lifted on to the quay for refitting and barnacle-scraping. As the convoy wound into the port, they became aware of the grim fort above them. With its six guns pointing out of embrasures commanding the Channel, this surrounded a massive rock formation, and dominated the harbour from the west side.

Ken reported at once to the battery commander, who arranged to house his team of beachcombing mine-hunters. As usual, they got straight down to work next day. To reach the east wall of the harbour, from which they were to operate, Ken had to borrow a whaleboat from the naval authorities based upon the peace-time London-Paris Hotel there. Although the port looked different in its present garb, it still reminded Ken of pre-war scenes he had watched on newsreels, as the Newhaven-Dieppe boats carried celebrities to or from France.

Dressed in denims and carrying their precious mine-detectors, marking-tape, and other tools, they climbed down the vertical ladder on the harbour wall into the whaleboat and pulled across the mouth of the port to the tip of the east wall. On the first morning, Ken made this their daily headquarters, as from it he could make a quick visual reconnaissance of the area to be cleared.

At that initial moment, he shielded his eyes against the glare from the sun on the sea, and picked out clearly for quite a distance the tops of two rows of beach mines in staggered formation. Fanning a detector as it dangled below the wall, Ken lowered himself carefully down to the sand and started to walk. The imprints from his feet marked his course as he continued to swing the detector ahead of him in a wide, thorough arc. There was no telling that the rows of mines visible represented all which were there, for laying charts could not always prove accurate on beaches affected by the sea.

Soon he had reached the first few mines in the two rows. Scraping with supreme care around their perimeter, he exposed, then lifted them, one by one – finally extracting their lethal little fuses. These were Royal Engineers' mines containing eight pounds of explosive, but from Ken's point of view would be just as dangerous as the bigger beach mines. They could be set off if only light pressure were applied to the head of the spring-loaded striker pin, which pierced a detonator in the body of the mine. So, a slight slip in the sand would be more than enough to kill.

However, the section survived that first batch to reach the next one farther along the beach. This group were not so simple, as the sand and shingle of three years since they were laid in 1940 had covered them completely. They used their same system of detecting, marking, exposing, defusing, and carrying back to the harbour wall along the safe-lane between white tapes – and rendered the whole lot safe without loss.

Only one thing bothered Ken: how to dispose of several hundred defused mines. The difficulty eventually resolved itself with the help of the Royal Navy. The naval officer, Lieutenant Steele, who had assisted Ken in his arrangements for clearing the beach, now rose to the occasion again.

Steele was the Rendering Mines Safe officer for the area, which involved tackling any enemy – or British – sea mines washed ashore. Naturally he knew the skippers of the flotilla of minesweepers stationed in the harbour, and he introduced Ken to one of them. The skipper in turn invited Ken on one of his sweeps for magnetic mines along the Channel, saying that they could kill both birds with one stone.

At first light next morning Motor Minesweeper 119 rolled out of Newhaven harbour into a badly behaved Channel. Turning westward under the eye of the giant fortress, she plunged into the full face of a sou-westerly gale. Her bows rose to an alarming angle, stayed momentarily silhouetted against the stormy sky-line, and then dived into the dark troughs below. Ken clutched the rail of the bridge with his whole strength as each wave passed and plunged them down again.

Ken saw the helmsman for'ard and slightly below him spewing miserably as he hung on to the spokes of his wheel, and fought to keep his feet as spray swirled over the deck. Ken could not have been ashamed at feeling ill himself if an experienced helmsman was actually sick in such a storm. In mid-Channel the motion thankfully became more rhythmic, regular, although the minesweeper was still pitching pretty badly.

Then Ken had a second surprise as the skipper said quite calmly, "Think I'll go below for breakfast. Keep an eye on her, Revis, will you, while I'm gone? You want to keep to the port side of that buoy." His fingers pointed to a blur barely visible in the distance through strong field-glasses!

Good thing the helmsman knew his job, Ken thought, as he stood there in apparent command of a motor minesweeper. He even gave a few hastily learned orders down the speaking-tube, which seemed to be obeyed well enough. Then he went below for his own breakfast when the skipper returned, and kept it down by tossing back half a tumbler of Navy rum afterwards.

The sweeper was on a routine search for magnetic mines, but Ken felt more concern for his own mines. For, of course, he had brought his defused mines with him and stacked them on the deck aft. His plan was to dump as many as he could overboard when the skipper

47

told him that they were in a sufficiently deep part of the Channel. Any he could not get rid of in a safe depth, he would try to detonate. So, Ken was busy hurling the mines over the stern of the sweeper as it ploughed on its course, and he disposed of most in this way.

For the remainder, he had brought a coil of slow-burning fuse that was unaffected by water. He attached a short length of this fuse to the detonator of each mine, and inserted the detonator into the pocket of the mine itself, securing it with insulating tape. A hand's length of fuse burned for about thirty seconds, so Ken had time to light the fuse, hurl the smoking mine over the stern of the vessel, and wait for the bang.

As he released the first one, he did not know quite how long the fuse would take to burn, or how deep the mine would sink before detonating. But he soon learned. A crack like a twelve-bore gun growled out of the water, and the ship shuddered under his feet. That was only eight pounds of explosive at a range of about five hundred feet through water. Ken recovered from the convulsion and hurled another overboard, then another. From the general effect, he could imagine too well the shattering sound a depth-charge would make exploding below the surface, and felt quite glad he was an Army, not a Naval, officer. They nosed into Newhaven that evening, however, having dumped or detonated all Ken's mines.

Ken had not seen Jo since starting on mines, but before leaving Newhaven he thought they might get a day or two together, now that the beach was virtually clear. And as it happened, two days after his day at sea was her birthday, so she came down for the night on 12 August, and they stayed at a small guest-house near the harbour. When Ken met her at the station she looked as lovely as ever, and in her arms nestled a wonderful woolly Alsatian puppy.

Jo announced to Ken, "She's your birthday present to me!"

Unfortunately, Sheba was not yet house-trained, and the landlady left them in no doubt about her opinion of the puppy before they left next day! Ken saw Jo off after her brief birthday visit.

Having handed over a clearance certificate for the beach, Ken planned to move the detachment on to Pegwell Bay, in Kent, and took his leave of the battery commander at the fort and the other friends he had made there. The Revis convoy was on the move again, over the swing bridge beneath the shadow of the great gyn legs. Beachy Head, Eastbourne, Hastings, Folkestone, Dover, and, at last, Pegwell Bay. The vehicles found good cover under the trees at the rear of an inn called The Sportsman, where they pitched camp and set up a field kitchen for the evening meals after work.

Ken's orders here were to clear a section of beach between two breakwaters. The work went smoothly and without mishap. But Pegwell Bay has one of the shallowest beaches in the country, and the tide used to appear from nowhere, race in the last few hundred feet in a minute or so, and creep up behind the section as they swept. Several times as they were spread out in their usual safety-precaution line, the water swirled inshore of them without their noticing, and the first they knew was when it swamped their boots. This sudden inrush of sea could have made sweeping for beach mines nastier than usual, but the worst they suffered was wet feet.

At this period one job followed another without a break, and almost before they had completed the Pegwell Bay operation – admittedly a minor one – Ken's section was summoned to a more serious situation at Folkestone.

Driving through Folkestone itself, they went on to Shorncliffe, where Ken was to report to the O.C. of a field company, Royal Engineers, Major Hawkins, the inventor of the 78 Hawkins anti-tank grenade. Hawkins had agreed to billet Ken's troops, and met him at Shorncliffe with a business-like handshake.

"This is the gen, Revis. One of my subalterns has been blown up, and he's gravely wounded. He was sweeping for the first few mines, near the harbour. As soon as I reported it, I got orders to suspend operations and wait for you chaps."

Ken had already heard that Bomb Disposal sections experienced in beach mines would be replacing other units at present clearing them. And he had heard, too, that casualties in several places were rather alarming.

Ken was at the rendezvous next morning waiting to meet the new commander of No. 2 Bomb Disposal Group, Lieutenant-Colonel R.G. Marshall, R.E. Ken looked into the dark crater and twisted railway metals where the young field-company officer had been blown up. At that moment, the new commander's Humber Snipe drove towards him along the deserted harbour road and stopped near a glass shelter. Ken stepped forward and saluted. The Colonel sprang out, returned the salute, and said in a soldierly way, "I'm Marshall. This is the Chief Engineer."

The Brigadier, Colonel, and Ken moved into the shelter, where they spread out the large harbour plan showing the location of mines. The troops responsible for anti-invasion measures had done their job thoroughly in this vital area of Folkestone, for not only the railway track running into the harbour station but the adjacent beaches and the forecourt of a large hotel had all been laid with naval beach mines.

"When you've completed their clearance," Marshall told Ken, "report back to me. I'll be entrusting you with rather a special job, involving some booby-traps." Then, with a brief "Good luck," he was gone, taking the Brigadier with him.

They started on the railway line, but found this complicated by the interference of the mass of metal on the detectors' headphones. Safety first was always the order, so the operation slowed down considerably. Some of the mines had become jammed right under the rails, so Ken had to blow up these where they were. The sappers ran the electric cable across the road, and took cover in the small basement of a disused building near the track. Then Ken pressed the exploder plunger from the same spot – and the nerve-wracking noise echoed round the whole area. Earth and shingle settled, and they returned to the scene for the next one. So, it went on till Operation Boat-Train – as they nicknamed the job – was completed, except for the disposal of the mines Ken had dismantled rather than detonated.

Next day Ken took two lorry-loads of mines to the desolate inland St Martin's Plain. As a treat for the sappers, and by way of training in demolitions, he made sure that the rank and file had their chance to lay charges and detonate the mines by all the methods used in the Army. By general agreement they voted it a splendid half-day, spent amid the din of exploding mines, the whine of flying splinters, and the smell of spent gas and smoke.

A dispatch rider arrived at Shorncliffe that evening with a message for Ken to attend a conference at Group H.Q. on the following day at Tunbridge Wells. Ken could not know the significance of the summons. He drove up there as ordered and found Colonel Marshall presiding, with the Deputy Commander, Royal Engineers, Major Behrendt, M.C., Ken's own company commander, and several of the section commanders. After a general discussion on progress of the many mine-clearance operations from the Isle of Wight to the Thames Estuary, Marshall announced one or two changes in command and the assignment of new duties to some subalterns.

Then Ken learned what the special job was which Marshall had mentioned before the Folkestone operation.

"Revis, I want you to go to Brighton again and get rid of all the explosive devices from the Palace Pier and the West Pier."

Ken heard how the two famous piers had been festooned with mines, booby-traps, and naval depth-charges by Canadian engineers on their arrival in Britain during the early days of the war. It was with the plans of the pair of piers rolled up under his arm that Ken left the commander's room. From the quaint old corners of Tunbridge Wells, it would be first stop Shorncliffe, second stop Brighton.

Chapter 5

THE BLINDING FLASH

They saw smiling faces and friendly waves as the convoy wound through the gateway into Preston Barracks, and they made their way to new quarters. Ken was well known there by now, for this would be his third stay. He looked forward to the extremely comfortable officers' mess and meeting old friends again. And as the mess had been built just before the war, he knew his men would be well quartered. Ken reported to Major "Tiny" Milner and met a mixed bag of officers: infantry, gunners, sappers, Royal Army Medical Corps, Royal Army Service Corps, chaplains, and even Canadians.

Mines, booby-traps, and depth-charges – these were the three types of deadly devices bristling all over the two piers. Ken decided to take the Palace Pier first. He knew by now that the depth-charges on this pier were wired to an exploder in an underground room of the aquarium. This lay a little east of the shore end of the pier, and the only key to that tiny room and the handle of the exploder were kept in the custody of the town major, a breezy, kilted Scotsman, Major Morrison.

If Britain had ever been invaded, the small box in that room could have sparked off a charge at the end of the pier enormous enough to blow it to bits. Luckily the Germans never landed on the famous strip of sand between the two Brighton piers – or anywhere else – and the depth-charges did not have to be exploded. Now Ken had the job of dismantling the devices. He signed for the key and the handle, thanked Morrison, and left.

Ken made his way to the aquarium, and in the strange atmosphere of the place let himself into the silent room below the ground. He glanced round at the bare walls and then saw it. The box stood on a rough bench, with wires leading from its terminals away through a hole in the wall, and its plunger handle lying ready alongside. Not only quiet, the room felt icy cold to Ken as he unscrewed one of the terminals and removed its wire from the exploder, then the other terminal with its wire. That was easy enough, he thought, as he emerged into warmer air, blinked at the early September sunlight, and clutched his precious exploder box. He could not imagine this ever getting back into the engineer stores of the First Canadian Division.

No one had trodden the deck of the Palace Pier for three and a half years. Ken decided it would be wisest to make a first reconnaissance by boat, so two elderly Brighton fishermen and a craft were procured, and they all set off from the Banjo Groyne. The main end of the pier had been severed from the shore by a gap of about a hundred feet, leaving an island of metal stranded out to sea. Its only connexion with the shore was the electric cable between the exploder and the depth-charges located under the concert-hall of the pier.

The two oarsmen rowed with solemn faces as the boat heaved over a slight swell towards the 'island.' Ken noticed that the metal uprights supporting the island were each encased in several rows of one-pound guncotton slabs, and as the boat bobbed nearer still, he made out a wire winding upward from each leg into the gloom on the underside of the decking. He presumed that these also formed part of the anti-invasion system for blowing the pier from the shore, and realized that he would have his work cut out to cope with everything on these two Brighton piers.

After they had made a complete circle around the pier, they returned to the east side, where Ken told the boatman to close in to allow him to get on the pier. Before he left them, he told them to return at once on a signal from him. Ken wanted to get that settled, since the two men had been very loath to take him right to the pier in the first place, and let him know that they thought his chances of returning to dry land again extremely remote. With that comforting thought, Ken managed to get a foothold in the angle between one of the legs and a diagonal cross-bracing beneath the pier, and jerked himself free from the boat, which moved away at a smart speed.

So, Ken was on his own. For a moment as he got his breath back it all seemed slightly unreal to him – perched on a strut under the Palace Pier. In the distance he glimpsed the motley of mixed facades ashore: Regency, Georgian, Victorian, modern.

Then he returned to reality. A flight of iron steps running right from the sea up to the deck looked tempting, but he realized this obvious way of walking on to it would be fatal, for his plan showed some small dots there that he knew to be anti-personnel devices. He had no idea what kind they were, nor how he would tackle them if he had to.

Instead, Ken started scrambling about on the filthy barnacled lattice work between the sea and the underside of the pier. He clambered through a maze of metal joists, cross-bracings, water-pipes, drain-tubes, and cables of all sizes, and the water washed steadily a few yards below. The physical effort involved was all he could muster. Wherever he could get a foothold, he steadied himself and removed the detonators and primers from the guncotton slabs on the uprights within reach, and he also somehow managed to hoist himself high enough to get at some of the fuses of the mines laid beneath the teak footways. Dismantling these in an uncomfortable position, after they had been exposed to the weather since the spring of 1940 or earlier, could hardly have been more awkward or dangerous.

When he had done all he could below deck, Ken decided to take a look on top before he left on that first visit. All the time he had been working underneath it – for more than two hours – he had a coil of rope wound about him which constantly got in the way: now it came into use. He took it off and with great difficulty made one end fast over the deck handrail. Then he hauled himself up on the rope, already very tired, till he hung on the sea side of the handrail.

Somehow, he gripped the base of this railing and held on. An inch at a time he raised his body, and at last when he felt exhausted, he drew level with the base of the railing. One heave and he pitched over the handrail on to the bench the other side. As he looked down the length of the pier, all he could see was desolation and decay. Paintwork peeled off, metal corroded, wood and cardboard littering the deck. The concert-hall had once gleamed gold and white; now it looked like a mausoleum, with its open doorways and dimness within. All Ken heard was the sound of the sea. Nothing more remained for him to do yet, so he recalled the reluctant rowers and stepped safely on to Banjo Groyne despite their gloomy forecast.

While Ken was making his first reconnaissance of the island part of the pier, his sergeant and the rest of the section began the job of erecting a tubular scaffolding pylon near the southern end of the other portion. A similar structure then had to be built on the island portion. Then they used a large pulley and a hook to connect the two by a fall of rope, under which they slung a small wooden seat for hauling men or stores. This contrivance worked well as a kind of sea-lift, and it also enabled them to bring back any of the smaller mines and fuses that could be carried by hand. Though the prospect of crossing that hundred-feet stretch suspended in a seat with an armful of mines could not have been ideal.

When the bridgehead had been completed the job really began. The main bulk of the hidden charges seemed to be concentrated in the concert-hall, according to Ken's plan, so he decided to clear the mines along the right-hand side of the approach to it until he felt he could claim sufficient area. Then he brought one or two of the men over to help organize returning the used stores to the landward side. Ken and an N.C.O. worked on this stretch, above and below the deck, until they reached the hall itself. Then Ken decided it was up to him to avoid as much danger as possible to the men.

"Wait here," he told the sergeant. "I'm going to have a look around inside."

Ken moved towards the bar first, treading carefully on the most solid parts of the floor just inside the door jambs. Booby-traps could be right in the middle. Everything was deadly quiet, uncanny.

A round metal tray advertising a pre-War cider caught his eye as it lay on the floor about halfway between the door and the foot of the counter.

Ken's mind flashed back to a day nearly two years earlier when he had been on a booby-traps course at Ripon. His instructor had rigged up a house supposedly recently occupied and abandoned by the enemy. He had watched while a British patrol came along, delighted to find somewhere to rest. A lance-corporal went in first. A picture hanging crookedly on the wall attracted the N.C.O. and he went to straighten it. He set off a booby-trap which would have killed the whole patrol, though in the demonstration it only produced a pistol-like shot. Then they were only playing at it. This was real.

Ken tiptoed across to the tray and knelt with his eye nearly on the floor. He squinted under it but could not see anything, so gently slid the blade of his long knife beneath until the tray eventually rose an inch or two. No bang. No booby-trap. Nothing except a circular patch of damp on the neglected parquet floor.

Ken did dismantle several devices of one sort or another, however, as he cleared a way painstakingly through the bar and into the amphitheatre, marking the route as he went with chalked symbols.

Once inside the amphitheatre, he looked from the back of the hall, where he stood, down the sloping floor towards the stage. He saw at once, with a trained eye, that the floor-boards appeared to be very uneven and the carpet over part of them far from flat – as if it had been kicked aside.

This gave him a clue, and he soon found the first of the depth-charges roughly as marked on the plan, under the floor by the corner of the building. Ken looked down at it, surprised at its size and shape, which reminded him of a big black tar-barrel. Ken went on to find all four of these depth-charges, intended to blow up the pier in emergency, and later had the help of Lieutenant-Commander Riley, R.N.V.R., in removing their fuses. This officer was attached to the section during the time when naval armaments were expected.

Eventually Ken cleared the whole of the Palace Pier, with the assistance of his section and the naval officer. Every swing door, every tip-up seat, every floorboard was safe again. And it had all been done without loss. Ken made a final thorough inspection to see that no booby-traps had been overlooked, and then he climbed over the arched roof of the amphitheatre, surveying the pier and the town like a conqueror. Which, in a way, he was.

The last things to be taken off the far end of the pier were the four deadly depth-charges, whose weight presented a problem. In place of the home-made bo'sun's chair they used two breast-lines. Then the party slung the four-hundred-pound drums – one by one – under the hook with timber hitches. As they wormed each depth-charge over the gap with an improvised winch, the carrying rope sagged in the centre, but they nursed the great drums across until the fourth one was at last lowered to the deck at the land end of the pier.

Palace Pier done; West Pier still to do. Meanwhile Ken enjoyed a week-end of wonderful weather with Jo at Robin Young's home. For a day and a half almost continuously, they lay on the lawn under the large dark cedar-tree of the Surrey garden. Then it was over. Before starting on the second pier, Ken made a reconnaissance on Portslade beach, near Brighton, obeying orders to give a start to a section under the command of a lieutenant who had not yet tackled a live minefield. Then came the West Pier.

Never had there been so strange a reason for anyone to traverse the promenade between the Palace and West Piers. It was only a short way for the men and trucks, but before they could approach the forecourt of the second pier, they had to pull aside two aprons of barbed wire and several coils of concertina wire.

Ken set up his daily headquarters at the forecourt, as the most convenient place, and then set off for a reconnaissance with his section sergeant. They pushed through the rusty, creaking turnstiles at the entrance, and were on the landward part of the pier. Ken was immediately attracted by a miniature car-racing track, where tiny Monopostos were still stacked away on raised benches waiting for the day when they could be wanted again. All the automatic machines still stood there. No one minded What the Butler Saw, nor had the Prison Hanging-scene been enacted since 1939. Ken looked into a Crystal Ball in passing, but saw nothing.

He and the sergeant then moved out to the open air and advanced carefully along the pier, eventually reaching the gap. Torn timbers projected like fangs from their shore-side of the pier as they gazed across at the second 'island' out there, with cast-iron legs and a load of lethal explosives. They would have to use the bosun's chair again to get across the gap so Ken left his sergeant to arrange erecting the tubular scaffolding for this shore end of the ropeway, while he went off to find his two wary boatmen at Banjo Groyne. After the surprising success of his first mission, they seemed slightly happier to take him out to the West Pier.

The same system this time. Ken clambered on to the under-structure of the pier where he located two or three beach-type mines tucked away inconspicuously, and defused them on the spot. After ascertaining that there were none at all near the gap end of the island, he felt he could authorize a ferry service for the stores needed to link the pylon on this part of the pier. They were already well established here by evening. Everything seemed to be much the same as on the previous pier, and Ken spotted one of the depth-charges from a short exploration farther along under the decking, while waiting for the first stores to arrive. He saw no reason why the operation should not be half over by that time next day.

As a final precaution before going off duty, he approached the commanding officer of a Royal Australian Air Force unit billeted in one of the hotels opposite the head of the pier, and asked if a picket could be posted on the shore side of the gap to prevent anyone approaching the pier.

10 September dawned bright, but the sea heaved under the pier. Ken dressed in his normal battledress blouse and trousers. On each shoulder, his two pips set in a surround of navy blue; a little lower, just below the shoulders, the red flashes of the Royal Engineers; and adorning the left sleeve, a gold bomb on a red oval. Gaiters and boots completed the uniform, apart from his peak cap. Ken could never stand the straight cheese-cutter type of cap, so he had taken out the normal stiffening circle to make it floppier. By now it had become really bent, and even acquired the nickname of his 'Luftwaffe cap.'

The sun still lay low to the south-east as he drove down to the pier head from Preston barracks. Ken breathed the morning air deeply. It was good to be alive; to watch the sun on the sea.

"Four of us will be enough for this – two parties of two each," Ken said. "When we get across, Marnock and I will keep to the right of the hall, and you two to the left." Corporal Marnock, the lance-sergeant, and lance-corporal nodded.

The bosun's chair was rigged all ready, and Ken got into it first. Away went the pulley wheel as he swayed out over the water until he dangled in the middle. Then the sappers hauled on a return rope and he travelled the upward half of the journey much more slowly. As the chair jolted towards the end of the ride, Ken lifted his feet clear of the boards, felt for the deck with them, and was out of the seat in a second. The pulley went back and brought the three N.C.O.s over one at a time.

Ken concentrated on helping them land, but as soon as they were all across safely, he got out his plan of this end of the pier. Their targets were small anti-vehicle mines with an ordinary spring-loaded striker which forced itself into the detonator cap and fired with slight vibration applied to the circular cover plate. Although these were normally used as anti-tank mines, they had been laid under the deck here as anti-personnel weapons, to catch any enemy troops landing on the pier.

Then the four of them split up into pairs as arranged, with Ken and Corporal Marnock taking the right route, and the other two the left. Each party had a plan showing the positions of the mines, and as Ken came up to where the first one should have been, he saw a small blue spot about the size of a match-head painted on the decking. This had faded with weathering but was still visible, and presumably marked the location of the mine, though the plan did not mention it.

Ken called across to the other pair, "We've got a blue mark where the mine ought to be. Look and see if you have, too."

A pause, and then the lance-sergeant confirmed that they had.

"Well, this is the place on the plan. Better go ahead."

Ken and Marnock took up the deck and there lay the mine. Ken defused it, put it on the deck, and told the others to carry on.

10 a.m. Now they were in a world of their own, an island far from the green Southdown buses that threaded along the front. They worked on quietly, with only an occasional phrase. Both pairs had defused several mines and rounded the corner of the hall out of sight of each other. Six safe mines lay behind Ken, marking his course down the deck. He checked the chart for number seven, and then looked for the blue spot. He went down on both knees to find it, his body bent. His back ached a bit by now, so he straightened for a few seconds before starting to get the deck up. Still on his knees, Ken said to Marnock behind him, "It's money for old rope, this."

He bent down again and peered at the blue spot. Then he was statue-still.

At that instant it happened. Thirteen mines went up in the blinding flash. Ken collapsed. Part of the pier caught fire. In the swirling smoke the others could not find him. Eight minutes passed as he lay there. Then he came round. He thought it was the next second after the explosion.

"No light. Face burning with blood, pulp. Ears bursting. Din. Dark. Chaos. Strain to open eyes. Wreckage roars down. Mustn't go under. Pier gone. Feel face. In ribbons. Flesh and blood. Hand to chest. Blouse bloody. Quieter. Agony. Where's corporal? Must be dead. I'm not. Voice through my mouth. Help. Footsteps on the deck. Coming, sir."

Lance-Corporal Northcote raced round from the other side of the hall to help. He saw Marnock standing in smoke, dazed with shock, and Ken kneeling, hands to face.

"Maddening blackness. Hands under my arms now. On my feet. Left leg. Right leg. Who is it? Mustn't go under. Got to get to land. Walking with the voice. At the chair. Legs through the ropes, over the seat. Clinging to the seat, swinging down, and up. Voices at the other end. Confused. Half-heard. Raising my legs, hands tugging at boots. More pain. Wafted out of the chair. A nightmare now, passing out. Back – on a stretcher. Put your head down, sir. I do. The gap's behind me. Relief. Dry land. All right now. Stretcher jolts in step. Stops. Cover his face up, girl's voice says. I'm not dead yet. Take the bloody thing off.

"Wife's address? I reel it off. Swung into an ambulance. Purr away. Someone holding right wrist. Left one feels broken. Everything does. Hazy. Must keep alive. It's all right, relax, voice whispers. Injection. East Grinstead. East Grinstead. I know it will be. I know it."

Chapter 6

FRESH FACE ON LIFE

Jo was a remarkable girl even in those days. All the time Ken had been in Bomb Disposal she felt confident that nothing would happen to him. But now for the first time, with his summer leave overdue, a definite premonition hung over her during the early days of September. She could not identify or explain it, either to Robin Young or herself, but it was there all the time just beneath the surface of her daily life.

On the morning of 9 September, Jo went into Guildford to do some shopping. Next day, immediately after lunch, she sat down in the lounge to write to Ken. She had started to tell him about things at Send and what she had bought in the town.

Then the phone rang in the hall. As Robin was in the garden, she put the letter down on the arm of the chair and went to answer it with a strange feeling. Jo never did finish that letter. She caught the name Major Holland, and was sure.

"I'm afraid I've got very bad news for you, Mrs Revis. Your husband's had an accident. But he's alive."

Jo said something, she had no idea what. The voice went on: "He's gone to Brighton Hospital, and he'll be on his way to East Grinstead by now."

Jo heard the words "East Grinstead" in a haze. She and Ken had been to the Officers' Club there several times from Horley, and although she admired both the patients and the staff, she knew what it meant – plastic surgery. Holland gave her one or two more details, and then said good-bye to her.

She heard Robin coming up the steps. "It's happened," Jo said quietly to her. "I suppose I always knew it might." She did not cry.

Robin was helpful as ever.

"You go and pack a few things quickly while I ring for a taxi and find out about the trains."

59

Jo was only gone a few minutes, but by the time she came downstairs again, Robin had arranged it all, and the taxi was on its way from Woking. Numbed, dazed, Jo could only pray that Ken would live and his brain would not be affected. That was the danger she dreaded. The taxi arrived about 2.20, and she had no time to let Ken's parents know, but thought perhaps it was as well for the moment. Jo did not know then that it had taken four hours since the accident for her to be told.

Robin offered to go all the way with her, but Jo would not let her.

"No, I'll be all right, really."

So, Robin went to the train at Woking, and insisted on giving Jo some knitting to do on the way. The fast electric train threaded across the points and up to one of the centre platforms at Woking, and in a minute, Jo was being hurried to Waterloo. She stared out of the window occasionally, not taking in what she saw. The Sorbo factory just outside Woking; Brooklands track at Weybridge, now a war factory; Sandown Park racecourse at Esher; Surbiton, and the long, built-up miles to London.

The trains to East Grinstead were infrequent, and the one Robin had looked up gave Jo only a few minutes to get to Victoria. She ran to the taxi-rank at Waterloo and said to the driver, "Look, my husband's had an accident and is in hospital. I must catch the train from Victoria in ten minutes' time. Please try and do it. Crash any traffic lights you have to – and I'll pay any fines."

"That's all right, lady, we'll fix it."

He did, too, hurtling over Westminster Bridge, round Parliament Square, and down Victoria Street. Jo jumped out in front of the station: "Thank you very much."

She offered a ten-shilling note, but he would not take anything at all. So, into the train with a couple of minutes to spare. That part of the journey was the worst, with a compartment full of wooden-faced people all around her. She was glad of Robin's knitting in the next hour or so.

In the taxi from the station to the Queen Victoria Hospital, she thought of Ken, but could not really get to grips with the situation, nor imagine what to expect. The sight of the building, looking like a cottage hospital, somehow made her feel that everything would be all right, and the staff seemed to confirm this as she was taken to meet the Sister.

"The surgeon will be with you in a minute."

This was one moment she would not forget, waiting for the surgeon's first verdict on Ken. He came in, and seemed exactly right for his job in every way, not that Jo was conscious of analysing him just then.

"Mrs Revis, I'll be frank. Your husband is in a very bad way. Fortunately, he's as fit as possible. The pulse and heart are good – but we fear very much for his eyes."

Once more, Jo scarcely had time to take in the full significance of it on the spot.

"What about his brain?" she asked.

"There is no need to worry about that. It does not seem to have been affected at all. The eyes are the worst worry. I've contacted Mr Ridley in Town, and he'll be coming down at once. We'll operate later to-night. Now, how about you? Are you all right? He's not under drugs or anything, so if you'd like to see him for a few minutes I'll arrange it at once."

"Yes, thank you," Jo heard herself saying.

Jo was shown along towards the ward, where she met Sister Meeley, who had that rare combination of efficiency and humanity. She told Jo, "Things are as well as can be expected. We were surprised just now when we were talking near his bed and he murmured to us. The only thing we've been able to do so far is clean him up."

Ken was in the end bed of the ward, the one nearest the Sister's small room. They reserved this position for the most seriously injured, so that she could get to it quickly if necessary. She later learnt that the famous flyer, Richard Hillary, had occupied it before Ken. Then as the Sister led her into the ward, Jo saw his face covered with a light gauze to keep the bandage in place across his eyes and mouth.

Faint, muffled sounds reached Ken as he oozed back to consciousness. They scarcely seemed to penetrate as he struggled to think what they were, where he was. He remembered the pier. And the crash. Nothing more. He felt a warm bed supporting him, but everything was dark, and he could not change it. A tight, singing sensation hurt his head so he raised his right hand upward from outside the bedclothes to feel it. What he found was his head hidden in bandages. He could tell, though, that his mouth felt open to the air. It also felt swollen and useless. As well as the pain in his head and shoulders, his left arm lay limp.

He hovered in this state for a while, until he heard a soft voice, "Your wife is here to see you, Mr Revis." Then he felt a hand placed gently on him.

"Hello, darling," Jo whispered.

"I've made a mess of it this time, haven't I?" Only his lips moved.

"Don't worry," she said.

"You got here quickly." Ken had no idea of the time, and did not know it was already past seven o'clock. Nine hours since the accident.

61

"I can stay a few minutes more," Jo said, "but I won't go far away. You're going to have an operation soon, about eight o'clock."

Ken felt confused but infinitely relieved that Jo had come and would be there from then on. He asked her, almost casually, where he was, and seemed to expect the answer.

"East Grinstead, darling."

He grasped the fact of the operation, also that he had been given blood and plasma to make up for what he had lost earlier. Ken drifted off again, with Jo still sitting there, and the Sister beckoned her away.

"We'll call you when we want you, Mrs Revis. And we'll let you see him as soon as possible after the operation. Now you go along to have some supper." To her own surprise, she did so, and then played cards with one or two of the night nurses. Jo still felt no outward reaction; she was still too numbed to show anything.

But she would certainly have shown shock if Ken's face had not been covered when she saw him. For, although he had been cleaned up and stitched a bit at Brighton before reaching East Grinstead at 4.45, his wounds were severe and his face almost unrecognizable.

At eight o'clock they began operating upon Ken. The operation lasted for hours. At the staff's suggestion, Jo went to bed at about quarter past eleven with a sedative, and, to her surprise, fell into a deep sleep. She was awakened between 2 and 3 a.m. by a nurse.

"You can come and see your husband for a minute now, Mrs Revis."

Outside, a thunderstorm added to the nightmare as she put on her housecoat and followed the nurse. To reach Ken's ward they had to go out under an open corridor, and the rain hammered down on its roof and blew in underneath. Jo tried to think she was reacting normally, but everything seemed so abnormal that she stopped thinking altogether. She seemed to be somewhere else, looking down at herself walking to the ward in the middle of the night.

Coming out of the storm, Jo saw the only light in the ward around Ken's bed, and beside it the apparatus for blood transfusion. For some reason, this comforted her, and she again felt things would be all right now that the operation was over.

"He's not likely to come round," the night nurse told her, "but he survived the operation well. Five or six hours, it took."

But at that, Ken stirred and shifted his head. The nurse and Jo were still whispering, and moved nearer the bed. He managed to ask the time.

"About three in the morning, and you've had a long operation," the nurse explained, moistening his lips. "Try to go back to sleep now. Your wife's here with you."

Jo spoke to him and he was off again. She asked if she could sit up with him, but the nurse was not keen.

"You'll just be wearing yourself out, Mrs Revis. He'll sleep for the rest of the night now. And anyway, Mr Ridley is wanting a word with you."

The eye specialist met her in the Sister's room.

"I thought you ought to know that there's not much hope for his eyes. Perhaps a fifty-fifty chance of seeing the light of day, but nothing else. We'll know in about five weeks, when we take the bandages off. Meanwhile, all we can do is hope – and try to be patient. I'm sorry. I leave it to you about telling him or not at present. But it would be better for him not to know for a while at least."

So, Jo went back to her room, dropped her housecoat on the bed, and fell into a restless sleep. When she awoke in the morning, she opened her eyes slowly and thought: Where on earth am I? The room seemed strange, but then the whole thing came flooding back to her. Ken. Ken. She got up feeling that the end of their world had come, and although she knew there could not be much hope for his eyes, she still just could not believe that he would be blind. It was something she had never thought about before about seven o'clock the previous evening. Was it really only twelve hours ago? Both of them had survived several ages of experience on that disastrous day, 10 September.

Then Jo pulled herself together a bit. Ken might have died; they had that comfort. Or his brain might so easily have been hurt. At the moment she was only looking for ways to soften the blow. She did not yet feel fully prepared for a positive approach to the future. In any case, they would not know anything finally for five weeks.

The first thing that Jo did that day was to wire their respective parents: "Ken badly injured, East Grinstead hospital." So started her five-week vigil of morning, noon, and night nursing. She went straight to the hospital after sending off the telegram, and offered to stay and help look after Ken. As they were short of staff, the offer was accepted at once, and they fixed her up with a pleasant place to stay, with a coalman and his wife. Apart from the fact that the couple had put up relations of patients before, their house had the advantage of being very near the hospital, reached through a thicket. Jo got to know every foot of that path in the following weeks.

Back in the ward, the sounds of daytime drifted into Ken's ears: footsteps, men's voices, china and cutlery. Muted sounds still, though, making him wonder as he awoke whether he had been deafened by the explosion. He remembered that again. He felt his head with his right hand, as he had done before, but only got as far as the hard helmet of bandages. Slowly he drew his fingers across his eyes, but again the bandages covered them. Pulverizing pain stopped further thought, and someone gave him an injection.

The next time he awoke was broad day, though dark to him. He did not seem to be too conscious of things yet, so she said as little as possible about his injuries. She remembered Ridley's words, and soothed him.

Besides Jo's presence, Ken was conscious of a hot-water bottle warming his feet through what he supposed were 'operation socks.' Two things which worried him: why did he feel pain in his left thigh and why was his left arm so heavy? The arm was in plaster, so probably something had been broken, he thought, perhaps the wrist. He wondered how he could have held on to the bosun's chair, though, before concluding it must have been with his right arm alone. Then he wondered about silly, irrelevant details. Where was his battledress and his shiny brown boots? What did it matter, he managed to tell himself. He would not want them again yet, perhaps ever.

What did it matter? His battered, broken mouth felt dry and hot, so Jo soothed it with a trickle of liquid through a rubber tube. Luckily for her, Ken did not seem able or inclined to think of the future. His immediate need was to have her there, and to have his burning, stiffened, sore mouth moistened every few minutes during his spells of consciousness. Jo never left him.

She told him that the surgeon had spoken to her about the operation and said Ken had come through it well. When they brought him to East Grinstead he was not suffering from shock in the clinical sense. Ken was glad to hear her recount how his pulse had been normal. That recent battle course proved its use, after all.

The persistent pain in his thigh puzzled Ken at intervals during that first day, until the surgeon who had performed the plastic work on him came to visit him for the first time.

"Hello, Mr Revis." The voice seemed to come from someone bending right over the bed. "How do you feel now? We've tidied you up as best we could."

The surgeon said nothing directly about his eyes, nor did Ken ask. The surgeon went on, however, to explain how three of them had worked for hours on him in the night. Ken gathered that their first job was to get rid of the debris that had been flung into his face, eyes, and shoulders, and to keep him alive after losing a lot of blood. He then learned that some skin-grafting had been necessary for the back of his left hand and for his eyelids. The skin used for this highly delicate work had been pared from the inside of his left thigh, which Ken found to be bandaged. So that was why his thigh had been hurting. One minor mystery was solved, at any rate.

A problem to be faced in the future was Ken's nose, which had been smashed in so badly, but plastic surgery cannot be hurried.

As the awareness of feeling returned to his battered body and muddled mind, Ken began to sense the stifling effect of the warm weather on his tight dressings. To make it worse, the open wound of his mouth had been treated with some softening and healing jelly which started to attract flies to his head generally. As Ken could not get rid of them himself, the nurse improvised a muslin mosquito-net, which she draped over the head of the bed. This cured the flies, but reduced the flow of air still further.

The hospital prescribed an egg-and-milk mixture for him, varied by grapes. So, Jo spent her time preparing all his food. With the aid of the rubber-spouted feeding-cup, she gave him the egg and milk, which he swallowed in tiny quantities at intervals of three or four minutes. The grapes she skinned, seeded, and halved before putting them in his mouth.

One of Ken's first visitors in Ward 3 was his company commander, Major Holland. Jo told Ken later that he looked distressed when he first saw the bundle of bandages, but despite this his usual brisk manner penetrated to Ken. Holland assured Ken about his section, particularly Corporal Marnock. The N.C.O. had been knocked out by the blast from the explosion, but not seriously injured.

Holland said that all was well on the pier. He had gone there straight after the accident and cleared the rest of the mines not detonated already. An act typical of Bomb Disposal, which Ken appreciated even in his present half-conscious state.

Dutchy Holland came loaded, too, with bunches of grapes. He heard how Ken could eat only these and the egg-and-milk diet, so sent every spare man in the company out on a tour of the area with orders to call on all houses with conservatories or hothouses!

"I heard that grapes are all you can take, so I put in train a military operation to get them."

Eggs, too, were hard to get in 1943, but batches of these arrived at East Grinstead in the days and weeks following. Ken heard that a concert had been planned for the other end of the ward during the evening, and he had a hazy recollection afterwards of having his bed wheeled into an adjoining room to escape the noise. Another thing he learned later was that Hillary, a former occupant of that bed, had been killed after returning to the air after months of plastic surgery. Although Ken could not be expected to appreciate them for a few days, the men at

East Grinstead were all very remarkable, many with gruesome cases of badly burned faces and limbs. He would get to know them later, but Ken himself somehow never thought of the possibility of injury. He assumed that he would be 'dead or alive.' At present he felt neither one nor the other.

The parents of both Ken and Jo visited him soon after his first operation. Ken's father seemed broken, yet kept his usual calm state outwardly, but his mother, not unnaturally, was terribly affected. She could see no hope, nothing beyond his probable blindness.

Jo meanwhile had to cope with Ken, all the parents, and her own feelings. The one who helped her most was her father. He had always been wonderful with her, quite unlike a parent, and so she turned to him now. As they took a stroll for a few minutes in the grounds outside the ward, she asked him, "What am I going to do?"

"You're not my daughter if you can't cope with this."

Jo's small sister, Jane, surprised them all, however. At nine years old she went straight up to Ken quite naturally, and spoke as if nothing unusual had happened. And her feeling for him was to continue over the years ahead.

Another early visitor was the C.R.E. After seeing him, Marshall went straight outside with Jo, and they sat on the green bank in front of the gate to talk about things.

"He'd have been out of B.D. soon, you know," Marshall said, adding that he would do anything he could at any time. He asked if he could come over again and bring some of the other officers to see him. In fact, Ken might have left B.D. before that, if he had had his way. Jo told Marshall how, before the Colonel's time, Ken had felt he wanted to go abroad and actually see the enemy, as he himself put it. He looked on it as rather dull at times and a long way from the front line.

So, the family and friends came and went – and Jo stayed. For the moment, she tried to concentrate on just the immediate future. It was not easy, though, and every morning as she awoke the same feeling swept over her – the same sense of panic. This lasted until the situation began to become normal and she took the first steps in trying to live with it. Then she would pull herself together and get on with the inescapable act of living from day to day.

During these earliest days it was getting Ken better that mattered, and she decided that as long as he said nothing about his eyes, or asked her outright if she knew the prospects, she would not mention it yet. The right time would come, and by then they would both be better equipped to meet it. But the whole game was nearly given away one day.

While some of the family were with Ken and Jo, a blind man who had come down for treatment happened to be in the ward. He and his wife walked over to see Ken, and they chatted to him about various things before bringing up East Grinstead and Ken's own case. He knew about Ken's faint prospects and was literally just about to mention the words "St Dunstan's" when Jo managed to divert him by putting her finger to his mouth. She did not know if Ken realized – probably not – but it would have been disastrous for him to learn like that and in front of the family.

During one of Ken's sleepy spells, he had a call from General Reeve, who had taken an interest in his work on the beaches since the first days at Bracklesham Bay. Only later did Ken realize that he ought to count the General's visit as a distinct honour.

He was getting a steady stream of callers, including such celebrities as the late Clark Gable, who was in the U.S. Army Air Force, and Elizabeth Allan.

"You've a very pretty wife," she said, "I do hope your eyes will be well enough for you to be able to see her again soon." So did Ken. In the meantime, he had to be content with Jo's constant care, and there were other distractions in his recovery.

Early on, Sister Meeley told him that he would have to be prepared to have his face and shoulders dressed twice each day. Ken realized that he must be fairly badly damaged altogether what with his face, shoulders, left arm, and thigh.

He would never forget the torture of the torn flesh on his face being cleaned and dressed. To try to take his mind off it, his thoughts turned to the future, to some hope, but that seemed too uncertain. He dreaded the clink of the dressing trolley, too, because it became connected in some way with the question of when or whether his eyes would ever be better. He was an intelligent man, and as he recalled how he had been staring straight down at the deck covering the mine when it went up a yard from his face, he could not help wondering how his eyes could possibly have escaped.

He was told that his eyes had been buried, or covered over, during the first operation, and they would be able to tell him more when the bandages came off after five weeks. So, hope and logic alternated in Ken's brain, which was just as well, for it allowed him time to recover enough to have his next operation.

About half-way through those first five weeks, some of the swelling had subsided enough to reveal more debris deeply embedded just below Ken's right eyebrow, so he was wheeled away to have it removed. For the second time after an operation, he experienced that slow return from painless sleep, and found himself back in his own bed once more. Jo was there, of course, and in answer to his insistence on knowing what they had done she gave him all the details she knew. They came across an assortment of materials around his eye-sockets, removing a large piece of teak as well as some rubber and string. The wood presumably splintered from the deck, and could not have been a good thing to have around the eyes!

As if this were not enough for one operation, Ken also had preliminary work done on his nose. The explosion had forced this into his face, and so the surgeons took the first steps in rebuilding it by easing it outward to help his breathing. Ken had been finding some difficulty during those initial two or three weeks.

Once again, the helmet of hard dressings was fitted, and for the next few days he did not have to endure those agonizing daily dressings. In fact, Ken was quite sorry when the new surgery work settled down and the dressings resumed. His next small encouragement came a little later when his naturally quick-healing body beat the need for daily dressings on the thigh, his "donor area," as it was known when skin had been grafted from one part to another for plastic surgery.

After this second operation, Ken had a further strain to combat. He found that having to lie on his back with scarcely any movement of his head began to exasperate him. He could not help becoming obsessed with a craving to turn his body to one side or the other, and he would have given almost anything to have been able to curl up on his side for just five minutes, with his head in some other position than the cradle of pillows. The pain of the wounds on his face – and elsewhere – would only allow a slight sideways motion, as any pressure was unbearable.

The days passed tolerably as Ken lay listening to the activity in the ward, or to Jo talking, or his being occupied with dressings and food. It was when Jo eventually went back to the billet to sleep, and the ward assumed an appalling quiet, that he could not relax, and wanted to jerk his head all over the pillow. He seemed to sleep only after hours of waiting, resorting to sleeping-pills in the middle of the night when exhaustion finally got the better of him. Then he would go off into a drugged sleep, with his very tender 'tail piece' supported in an inflated rubber ring and enough pillows to prop him in a half-sitting, half-lying position.

But by the time the effects of the operation started to wear off and that thigh did not need its regular dressing any longer, he became revived and encouraged enough to demand his first bath from the surprised staff.

"And don't worry," he told them, "I can get up and reach it easily."

With the help of the staff nurse, Winnie, he was soon out of bed for the first time and almost supporting himself. She guided his rather tentative and feeble steps to the bathroom next to her cubicle, and then Ken lowered himself gently into wonderfully soothing warm water. The wholesome feeling he got more than compensated for the effort, and his entire body seemed far fresher, apart from his plastered left arm and bandaged thigh. A quarter of an hour later, Ken crawled back to bed on Winnie's ever-present arm, with a sense not only of being cleaner but having taken the first faltering steps back – or forward – to life.

Ken was not quite ready yet to get up regularly, and so the life of the ward went on as usual. Although he could not stop a sense of anxiety about his eyes, fortunately the ward was full of other seriously injured cases. A common courage and challenge seemed to be shared among them all, almost as if they had reached some sort of unwritten understanding that the best way to tackle their adversity was with a grin. In this way they helped each other enormously. In the next bed to Ken was Henry, an American flyer, who had lost both his legs.

The day came when Henry took his own first steps on his new tin legs, lurching the few feet between his bed and Ken's. Jo described it all to Ken, as the American, clad only in his shirt and under-pants, forced himself forward on the awkward limbs. The rest of the ward sent up a cheer and laid bets on how far he would get. Cruel and comic in turns: this was East Grinstead in autumn 1943. From the fun of those steps Henry returned to operational flying, just like Douglas Bader, and died. But not in combat with the enemy. He was choked to death by a chicken-bone lodging in his throat.

Though they would not admit it, Ward 3 at that time contained an amazing group of men. The bomber-squadron leader, Bill Simpson, had crashed in France, burnt his face appallingly, and lost his fingers. While Ken was there, Simpson's book *One of Our Pilots is Safe* had just been published, and caused a stir in the ward. Another Bill, a Guards' officer, had a similar voice to Simpson's, and the ward were always amused when Ken could not distinguish their daily greeting to him across the beds. Ken joined in the joke, of course, as much as anyone.

The Canadian boy Cooper, or Coop, as he became called, was in the midst of having a completely new nose, chin, and ear. The number of his operations already ran into dozens, and when Ken arrived Coop's pedicle-graft nose was the current pride of the ward. A pedicle is a stalk of rolled flesh and skin, partly excised from the donor area of the patient's body, and attached by one end to some other part, so that it shall be nourished by the bloodstream until it is taken a step nearer to where finally wanted. Coop probably had a pedicle joining his thigh to his wrist, which would be severed from the leg after some weeks' nourishment there. Then it would be attached to his face for the same vitalizing period before his arm could be cut adrift from it, leaving a soft mass of flesh attached to his face – later to be modelled into a nose.

This sort of human joinery has to be a slow and tedious series of operations, because not only must the new skin or flesh unite physically with the damaged part of the body, but there has to be a linkage of the many blood vessels on each side to prevent the new portion from withering, like the grafted branch of an apple-tree, that has failed to 'take.'

By this time, Jo had really begun to come to terms with things. She found that East Grinstead was as happy as a hospital could be, and approved of its attitude, which seemed to be: "You help yourself, and we'll help you." In fact, one of the outstanding contributions towards the success of the hospital as a means of curing its patients' disabilities was its total lack of senseless rules and red tape. They all agreed that McIndoe's team of superb surgeons, doctors, and staff could not have been better. But best of all was this method by which each patient could make the rules for his own conduct in the hospital, provided that they did not conflict with the continuity of treatment. And as might be expected, these privileges were scarcely ever abused in any way.

A daily ration of beer became one of the highlights in the hospital round, and after Ken's second operation as many as half a dozen B.D. officers often sat around on the edge of his bed, cheering him up and drinking a pint of beer. If the dressings trolley trundled on the scene, of course, they had to take their glasses with them and make themselves scarce for a while.

Colonel Marshall made regular visits, too, exhorting Ken to "Keep your tail up, old boy." Ken intended to do this literally as long as it remained as tender as it still felt!

It was from Jo, however, that Ken heard the numbing news that Karl Kenway, his section sergeant, Sergeant Gallaway, and several others had been killed by a beach mine exploding as they were all grouped around it. Dutchy Holland's company was really becoming depleted, and destined to be more so, for not long afterwards, Ken's old section lance-sergeant, Henley, was also blown up and killed, while in another incident a young subaltern, John Willen, died soon after the mine he was working on exploded.

The loss of Kenway and the others took Ken's mind right off his own predicament for a time, and he felt quite humbled by its impact.

More days, with dressings still very unpleasant, although Ken's mouth had healed so well now that he could eat a little solid food. Jo or the nurses spoon-fed him, because with one useless arm he inevitably made a mess if he tried to transfer food from a plate to his mouth.

"Just like a bird in a nest," one of them said, as she popped food into Ken's mouth. "Better this way than spring-cleaning the bed after you've had a shot, Mr Revis!"

Jo survived that first month, not only looking after Ken but going round the wards talking to the others and often reading to them, too. She wanted to tire herself out, and she succeeded. But the surgeon saw her one day and drew her aside.

"Look here, Mrs Revis, you really ought to have an evening out. In fact, you must. There are two boys here who need an outing, too, so I'd be grateful if the three of you would go out somewhere. It will do you all good."

Jo did not really want to at all, but after mentioning it to Ken, who agreed with the surgeon, she and the two went into the town and had dinner and behaved as brightly as they could.

About the middle of October, Ken felt sufficiently strong to climb a bit shakily into his spare battledress for an outing slightly farther than the bathroom. His original uniform had been cut away from him, blood-soaked. Now, in this pressed battledress, he walked very slowly along the corridor to sit by the fire for half an hour or so in the officers' common-room. Not much, but progress. And a day later, a little more progress. He walked on Jo's arm into the grounds outside the ward, where he could feel the warmth of the sun through the bandages. Together they sat on a bench and chatted quietly for a few minutes. The trees in the distance gleamed gold, but only Jo could see their colour. Ironically the sun was actually too strong for Ken, so that his head began to throb and he had to go back to bed for the rest of the day.

"Sorry about this, darling," he apologized, "but we'll celebrate my birthday next week somehow, shall we?" So, on Trafalgar Day, 21 October, Ken's twenty-sixth birthday, they invited Colonel Marshall and a crowd of the officers from Tunbridge Wells down to East Grinstead. The guests drove Jo and Ken out of the hospital to the friendly setting of a hotel lounge, where they all drank to the occasion. Already Ken's other senses seemed keener, as he was aware of the warmth of the room and listened to their conversation. He even managed a whole pint of mild beer before being driven back to Ward 3, tired but satisfied at something accomplished.

Jo realized that the time must be approaching when they would know finally about his eyes. There seemed to be no particular signs of its nearness yet, however, so she just went on as usual.

71

After Jo had left the ward one day, Ken lay on his back in bed when quite suddenly the surgeon came in.

"We're going to have a look at you now," he told Ken.

And almost before he had time to realize it, the surgeon was starting to unwind the bandages from his head. They had buried his eyes, he remembered their saying, to give them the best chance of recovering from the pressure of the blast. With the surgeon was Sister Meeley, and the layers lessened one by one.

Suddenly it dawned on Ken with a rush that this really might be the moment. Would he ever see again? His mind automatically turned to the times he had watched a similar scene in a film or play. This could be the moment of truth, but it was not happening on the stage or the screen. His eyes were the ones being uncovered. How had other people felt in the past? How was he feeling? He scarcely knew. He could only hope.

The surgeon worked on gently, till Ken could feel the cool air against his face for the first time since 10 September. Surely all the bandages were off? But blackness was all that met him. No trace of light. Nothing.

"I'm going to put drops into your eyes," the surgeon said.

Ken flinched as the cold liquid dropped into eyes, or sockets, or something. Then they replaced the dressing, and the day ended. Ken spent a night torn with troubled thoughts and doubts, and as usual could only tell that the next day had dawned by the sounds around him. That morning the same scene was repeated. The dressings unwound. The drops. The dressings replaced. Jo came in a little later than normal, and missed it, so Ken said nothing to her. There was nothing to say till he heard something for sure.

Jo had become friendly with Barbara Beddington-Behrens, a girl doing war welfare work in St John's at East Grinstead, and after lunch that day this girl made a point of seeing her.

"Will you come out and help me today?" She sounded quite definite about it, so Jo agreed, and they met later and went into the village.

Ken was dressed when Sister Meeley came to fetch him and walk with him to her room. Ridley, the eye surgeon, was sitting there as the Sister led Ken in front of him. Ridley got up. Ken heard the chair scrape, and then felt a hand on his shoulder.

"Mr Revis, we've given you light tests and tried everything possible, but I'm afraid we can't do anything for you. Do you think you can get used to never seeing again?"

Ken seemed stunned as he heard the words. In his heart he had known they would come, but he had not fully accepted it, could not really believe it. He said something.

72

Ridley asked if he thought he could take it. Again, Ken managed only a murmur. Still dazed, he was taken into the sitting-room to rest. Ken spent the grimmest fifteen minutes of his life alone in that room. He wanted Jo badly.

Jo's outing had all been carefully arranged, of course, down to the timing, so that when she returned to the hospital Ridley motioned her into the Sister's room, leaving Ken in his battledress still in the sitting-room.

"Sit down, Mrs Revis." Then Ridley repeated what he had already told Ken. "There's just nothing more we can do. I'm terribly sorry. I've broken it to him – he's over there. I suggest he lives out from now on with you, and comes in just for dressings. You can go and see him in a moment, but first of all I want to know how you feel?"

Jo had had no real reaction that Ridley could discern ever since he had met her, and it worried him. He thought it high time she showed some emotion, but did not want her to break down with Ken. There was only one way he could do it.

"Look, Mrs Revis, don't you realize he's never going to see your face again?"

That did it. Jo cried for five minutes before pulling herself together again.

"I'm all right now, thank you," she told the surgeon.

She walked across to the room and saw Ken through the open door, sitting in the big easy-chair. She paused, and then went straight up to him.

"Hello, darling," she whispered. "I know what you've been told."

"Yes, I'm afraid it's true – I've thought so for quite a time," Ken said calmly.

"I didn't want to say anything till we were sure – but I wouldn't have lied to you if you'd have asked me."

"It's all right," Ken said. "It wouldn't have done any good."

"Well, we're going to stay with Mrs Sartin from now on."

They stayed there for a second in each other's arms, then as Ridley came in and coughed, Ken took Jo's arm on one side and his on the other.

They wheeled out of the room in a line, strode down the corridor, and in a moment were walking along a path outside the hospital. Ridley kept up a flow of talk as they covered a couple of hundred yards or more down the path. Then Jo told them to go on without her for a few minutes. Ken heard her footsteps retreating down a gravel garden path, but Ridley went on walking him. After a while, they turned round, returned to the gate again, clicked it open, and got to the door

73

of the house, where Jo and Mrs Sartin were waiting. Jo had been living here ever since the first terrible evening.

Mrs Sartin was a big, motherly woman, and a treasure right from that first meeting. She gripped Ken's floundering hand with an intentionally cheerful welcome, half-pulling and half-ushering him up the steps into her little hall.

"Now come along in, Mr Revis, you'll soon get used to the house. I won't help you – I know you'd rather find your own way around. And presently I'll be bringing you both a nice dinner."

So right away, in those first few minutes at Mrs Sartin's house, Ken had to face the fact he had never really considered before other than theoretically – he was going to be a blind man. For he had only been up and about a comparatively short time. He could count the days easily, a fortnight or so. Things were happening thick and fast now, and here he was with Jo at his side, exploring Mrs Sartin's house, bumping into walls but recovering. Still stunned by the news broken that afternoon, Ken made a good show of going through the motions of meeting the challenge. He did not betray outwardly any of his real feelings, not even to Jo.

In fact, it was Jo who took the lead in that first hour or two till dinner. As they sat there after the tour of the house, Jo said, "How are you, Ken?"

"All right, darling."

"Well, I think we'll have to decide straight away that no one is going to interfere with you. You're not going to be babied. We'll help you all we can, but it'll be better if you try to do things for yourself."

"You're quite right, of course. I'm glad Mrs Sartin seems to understand."

Jo still sensed a tense air, however, but was not really surprised for a second. While they waited for the meal, they talked about basic ideas along these lines, and then Mrs Sartin brought in the meal. Neither of them really felt like it, and Ken scarcely touched anything till the lady burst out pleasantly, "And there's no point in me cooking for you if you're going to sit there moping." At that Ken made an effort to eat it, and she said, "That's better" approvingly.

After it had been cleared away, Jo switched the radio on, and by one of those queer coincidences someone started to croon a current song:

I have eyes to see with,

But they see only you.. .

Ken and Jo were sitting in opposite armchairs as tears started to soak through the bandage across his eyes and stream down his cheeks. He could still cry. Jo jumped over to him, and flung her arms round his neck. They wept together and then felt better. It was Ken who suggested discussing the future, and again agreed to Jo's plan of self-help for him. The tension broken, they talked almost brightly about getting the families down again or going up to see them for Christmas. That was still some way off, so it did mean that they had started to plan, not just live and dread from day to day. Now they knew the worst, things could only improve. As Ken heard the click of the light switch in the bedroom, he knew that for a while at least they were both sharing the same darkness.

Next day things looked a little brighter to Ken, and he had things to fill his mind. But best of all, he and Jo were together under the friendly roof of Mrs Sartin. First on the list came an appointment with the ear, nose, and throat specialist about his broken nose and a slight deafness in the left ear, where the drum had been affected by the explosion. From that time on, Jo took him to the hospital each day for his dressings and his daily ration of vitamin pills, with the added incentive of a talk to the patients still confined to bed in the ward. That was better than a tonic in itself.

It was actually as well for Ken that he still needed quite a lot of treatment to keep him busy and help pass these first weeks aware of being blind. He began to resign himself to the basic fact. Now other things still had to be done, the surgeon told him. "It's important now not to allow your eye-sockets to shrink, so something will have to be fashioned to support your lids."

Ken guessed what he meant, that the eye-sockets were empty. The surgeon went on to explain that his eyes had been punctured and smashed, and it had been impossible to save them. Ken would have to have the sockets irrigated several times a day to wash away the unpleasant discharge.

All these weeks later, Ken learned the details of the damage discovered and remedied in that first long operation. The accident had ripped both his eyelids up the centre, like a pair of curtains, and the surgeons had repaired these by a delicate grafting of new skin to preserve the original hooded shape over his diminished eyes.

Ken now had to present himself at the dental department of the hospital, where they had orders to prepare plastic shells for him to prevent the new wedge-shaped section of skin from puckering and to check the shrinkage of the unsupported eyelids and sockets.

These turned out to be 'eyes' shaped rather like a young, half-formed chestnut. The dental mechanic made these from acrylic resin, then still quite a new plastic, and many hours passed before these could be fitted. Ken's eye-sockets still hurt a great deal, and the difficulties of trial and error took time in such a delicate job. In fact, Ken lost track of his number of visits to the dental chair before these eyes became bearable enough to endure them in his sockets even for a minute. He could not get used to these horrible, makeshift artificial eyes, and two or three more weeks elapsed, with lengthening the wearing time daily, before he could stand them for a whole day. All the while, too, they had to irrigate his eye-sockets repeatedly.

Jo did not take to nursing easily, but had her first contact with these awful eyes as she helped the mechanic choose the shade of blue nearest to Ken's lost eyes. With the best tone settled, the man coloured the front surface of the shells with a special glazing, following one of Ken's more recent photographs as closely as he could. Ken knew that at this stage his eyes were serving a surgical rather than aesthetic purpose, and looked forward to the time when he would have healed enough to get more natural specimens.

Meanwhile, the frequency of his various dressings lessened, and he was actually encouraged to leave the atmosphere of the hospital for trips into East Grinstead when the weather was fine. After a few of these outings, this palled a little, and so a special day out to visit Robin Young at Send was awaited quite eagerly. Dutchy Holland sent his car and driver on a day that neither were wanted, and the khaki-coloured B.D. car cruised across country to Send.

Both of them felt overjoyed to meet Robin again, though they had their own individual emotions about returning to the house with the great cedar-tree. To Jo it brought that first phone-call back to her, as if none of the intervening days had happened. When she wondered whether Ken would live or not. Now she knew. For Ken it meant a homecoming. Robin's house had been the last one he remembered seeing, so it had its part in forging a slender link with his world of vision. The hospital and Mrs Sartin's house meant merely imagined places. Here was one he really knew, could visualize. Being able to find his own way into the familiar drawing-room and slide his hand up the curved banister rail meant more to Ken than they realized.

It confirmed that his world was still there, even though he could not see, and it would have to be felt for with fingertips groping in the dark, or heard with ears acutely tuned. For instance, he had made out the cobbled Guildford high street as the car came up its incline. But although it was good to get away from East Grinstead, the drive had tired Ken, and after lunch with Robin, he had a rest upstairs under the eiderdown in the bedroom he knew well from previous week-end leaves. From below came the half-heard murmur of the two girls' voices as they talked together, then he went off to sleep till tea-time.

That evening he was back at the hospital none the worse for their day out – in fact, psychologically better.

Both Ken and Jo are natural optimists with a sense of humour, and it was this which would be bound to come through and triumph in the end. December came in, and during it Ken had at least two chances to show that he could see the funny side of not seeing – after only a month or so. They were hoping it would be possible to leave the hospital completely by Christmas, so that they could go home to one or other of the parents. But this meant getting his discharge from the Army.

To do this, for some reason known only to the War Office, Ken had to be taken to Haywards Heath before a medical board. Ken actually felt both sad and amused alternately on that day, since it must mean the end of his war. The silly side arrived, however, when he was placed carefully in front of the members of the board, who were presumably seated in line ahead. After a long rustling of what he could only presume were his official Service papers, the chairman chose to address him.

"Can you see anything?"

Ken gave a suitably polite negative.

"What, not a damned thing?"

They must have had the East Grinstead report before them stating that both his eyes had been destroyed, so to some people the questions might have seemed not only silly but intolerable.

Ken, however, merely assured them on the point, when the chairman replied, "Category E, out, I'm afraid."

Ken could not help chuckling at this absurd scene on the way back to hospital. So now the formality was over, and the only obstacle to be negotiated before they could leave East Grinstead, would be the treatment of his eyes.

Jo went to ask about the chance of leaving in time for the holiday, and was told, "Yes, he can go home for Christmas if you can do these dressings."

But to Jo that practically seemed to be saying no. For 'these dressings' meant a major nursing operation to her, and one which, although she loved Ken so much, she did not feel equal to doing. As Ken's eyes were so tender, their empty sockets still needed continued cleansing. To do this involved removing the rather grotesque shells with an actual hook, and then irrigating the cavity beneath the eyelids.

The surgeon and sister said that she had to try – despite her involuntary protest at first. So, they showed her exactly how it was done. Until then no one except the hospital staff had seen the raw hollows hidden by the two shells and bandages. As Jo watched them swabbing the sockets, she wondered how she would be able to do it alone, but

77

they insisted. The worst part was the hooking out, yet, of course, she did it perfectly well after some practice under their supervision.

They decided it would be better to go to Jo's parents for the holiday, as they had more contemporary friends there but Ken's parents had been invited up there as well. So, a couple of days before Christmas, Ken and Jo said good-bye to the Sartins, thanking them for their help and understanding, followed by farewells and wisecracks all round at the hospital. They were driven to King's Cross for the Grantham train, and the railway transport officer had even received orders to post a guardsman to carry their baggage and conduct them to the train.

From the start, Ken had a phenomenal sense of direction. He learned within weeks to touch with his knuckles bent and not with outstretched fingers. At the start, too, Jo always made a point of orientating him for the whole house. It was no good just letting him feel two or three things in a room, and then expect him to know the place, so she always explained the geography of a house at the outset.

"We're in the hall now, it's left into the kitchen, down a corridor to the lounge leading off to the right. We're in the lounge now. It's oblong, with a fireplace on the short side at the left here, and a big window on the wall ahead of you." And so on.

When Ken's parents arrived at Sleaford they had last visited Jo's home nearly three years previously for the wedding. Naturally they had forgotten the layout of the house a little, and they were amazed after they rang the bell. Ken and Jo opened the front door and they stepped into the hall. With the greetings over, Ken said, "Come along, I'll take you upstairs and show you around. There's our bedroom. Yours is the next one. You remember the lavatory, and the bathroom is here, right next door. And these are your towels over the rail." They were staggered.

With all four parents gathered at home, Ken and Jo felt they could talk more freely about his blindness. Jo even recalled some of her worst moments at East Grinstead, which she had kept to herself till now. They wanted to get over to the parents that it had to be treated naturally and not hushed up. More vital still, as Jo said quite forthrightly, "We've got to say one thing here and now. You mustn't baby Ken. Don't do everything for him. He's got to learn to help himself. We're going to get over this and live as normally as we can. There's no reason why we shouldn't do most of the things we have always done. Some won't be possible. We'll accept that. But you'll be surprised just how much Ken will manage."

"Hear, hear," Ken added.

That was something they had to establish, and repeat, even at the risk of offending the families. Ken came first, but not by being mollycoddled.

So, Christmas came and went; a strange time that turned out brighter than it might have been. Jo's natural zest and spirits had a lot to do with this, and it was already apparent, particularly to her father, that the success of Ken's life would depend to a considerable extent on her ability to cope with the situation – as he had told her she would when he last saw her at East Grinstead.

Ken and Jo were grateful to accept the gift of his parents' car, which had been stored away since the start of the war, and they would be pretty sure to get a petrol ration to help him get about more easily.

The subject of cars reminded Ken and Jo of a very early meeting they had in those idyllic days at Sleaford during the summer of '39. They spotted a car chugging along the main street and emitting masses of blue smoke.

"That car's using a lot of oil," Jo said quite naturally, for her father had insisted she learn all about the inside of a car as well as its outside.

"*What* did you say?" Ken was overcome. A girl looking like Jo knowing how a car works!

Their will to win was soon seen clearly by the parents. Ken had already arranged to go to St Dunstan's for a course of training, when they heard that one of the local dances being held over the holidays was actually in aid of St Dunstan's.

"Let's go," Jo suggested.

"Well, why not?" Ken thought it seemed timely to put in an appearance, as it would give them a chance to try dancing together in these changed circumstances, while helping the institution he would soon know much better.

Until then, it had hardly occurred to Ken that a blind person could make much of an attempt at dancing, so he and Jo practised a few steps in the drawing-room before the evening. If any of the family were surprised, they did not show it. But no one could deny that this was a fresh outlook on blindness. Ken seemed determined to make a go of life, and dancing was one of the things he had always enjoyed. He remembered a dance back at Bedford when he made his first appearance as a singer; perhaps he would do that again one day.

Ken and Jo arrived at the dance, but although he enjoyed the experience, he found it a rather confusing one. He did not tell Jo he had a headache. It was giving him his first experience in steering by sound, however, and between them they managed without bumping into anyone. Ken located the band, and when Jo had told him the shape of the hall, he got on quite well. It was just that the general noise seemed excessive to him still.

During an interval, he was shown to the gentlemen's toilet. Ken was washing his hands at a basin when he heard a man next to him. For something to say, he just commented, "I don't think much of the band, do you?"

"Well, I'm playing in it!" said the man.

Ken tried to soften the blow.

"I really meant the piano accordion."

"That's what I play!" came the cool voice. One of Ken's first *faux pas*!

Back at home, despite Jo's warning words about too much attention, she had to shield Ken from an excess of loving care lavished on him. Mental torpor – that was what Ken wanted to avoid. And they had to conduct quite a campaign to see that he was not waited on hand and foot – nor prevented from even thinking for himself. To some one as active in every way as Ken, inertia and brooding in blackness were the main enemies. He seemed to be fighting both of them well, but he had to have help. Jo was wonderful in just the right way, even in these early days, by putting things within reach yet making him actually find them himself. If Ken wanted the radio, he would have to switch it on, though there were plenty of people willing to do it for him. Despite all her efforts, Ken still not unnaturally had a certain fear for the future.

It was to try and overcome this that he really decided to go to St Dunstan's. The organization meant little to him then, apart from what he had learned about it before leaving East Grinstead, but it became increasingly clear that he ought to train there, as so many others had benefited from it in the past. Perhaps it could solve some of his problems, or at least help him.

Ken had heard that the vicar of Rippingale, in Lincolnshire, was once chaplain to St Dunstan's, so went to see him. The clergyman was extremely encouraging to Ken, telling him that he had the spirit of St Dunstan's, and conveyed the impression that they did their best to avoid a man feeling sorry for himself. Already Ken was getting out of that frame of mind, but as yet had little with which to replace it.

The New Year opened excitingly, for a telegram told Ken and Jo that he had been awarded the M.B.E. in the Honours List. After that surprise, the next stage was St Dunstan's and learning to be blind.

Chapter 7

LEARNING TO BE BLIND

A new year and a new life. On a raw morning in early January 1944, Ken and Jo piled their possessions into the newly acquired car, wedging the big blue trunk right across the back seat, and set off from Sleaford. Jo's mother had prepared a vacuum flask of hot soup and some sandwiches for their lunch, and so, with Ken safely settled in the left-hand front seat, Jo aimed west-south-west out of her home town to Church Stretton, the evacuated headquarters of St Dunstan's on the other side of England.

Grantham, Leicester, and then the Watling Street highway for a while. The soup had kept as hot as when it was boiling in the saucepan at Sleaford. After lunch Jo wheeled westward into the hilly country of Shropshire, with all its quaint place names. Much Wenlock came and went, and the sweeping Shropshire sky-line passed, too, unseen by Ken in the amber afternoon. The mileage on the speedometer had risen by more than a hundred, and they were already beginning to think of tea when Jo reached the village of Church Stretton, near the Montgomery border, and suddenly saw one of the first signs of St Dunstan's. As she slowed down, she said, "We must be near it now, Ken. There's a young man with a walking-stick. He's feeling his way along a wire stretched out between some posts."

She could not be expected to know what those words meant to Ken. His heart froze for a second.

Am I going to be just one more like him – groping about for the rest of my life?

Despite his amazing optimism, Ken could not help this periodic panic. But he seldom showed it. The mood was often momentary, or, at any rate, short-lived, and now, as the car swung away from the main road, the trunk in the back bumped a bit at the sharp turn to distract him. Jo manoeuvred up a long steep hill till she found Tiger Hall, where they had to report.

81

But Ken still felt apprehensive as he slid his legs out of the car, took Jo's arm, and entered the hall of the large house. From then on, he hardly had a chance to consider how he felt.

"Welcome to St Dunstan's, Mr Revis," said Nurse Buckley, introducing herself and putting her hand in his to shake. "You're just in time for tea. Just leave your bags and everything – someone will look after them. Come in and meet a few friends."

Ken was already learning to use his other senses to their fullest. The first he felt in this room on the right of the hall was one of warmth from a fire. Welcoming warmth. Then they were introduced to Jack Tutin and his wife, Kay. Jack told Ken in an Irish voice that he was a St Dunstaner, too, but could see just a little. Lucky devil, Ken thought.

Then other sounds took charge. The clink of teacups, crackle of the fire, voices in the hall.

"That'll be Ed Dunlop coming in," Jack said.

But the next Ken knew was the door opening and a girl's footsteps entering first of all. Then an attractive Canadian voice announcing, "I'm Loraine Ericson. Glad to know you. Here's Ed Dunlop."

As the man approached, Ken heard his Canadian voice ask, "Got any hands?"

Some strange greeting used way out West, Ken thought, till he stretched out his hand and felt a fingerless stump. An early lesson to Ken that there are always people worse off than oneself – a valuable lesson as well.

That first tea-party seemed gay enough to Ken, with plenty to talk about – even if the sound of new voices was always a bit hard to identify. And confusing to Ken, too, as he did not yet know how long he would be staying in that house; how long Jo would be with him. He still depended on her too much. It could not be otherwise. But by the time he had experienced the full St Dunstan's treatment, a lot would have happened. Just then, a soft feminine voice said that it belonged to Matron Pain.

"You'll still be needing treatment to those eye-sockets of yours, Mr Revis, so we've arranged for you to stay here at Tiger Hall for a few days." This was the hospital of St Dunstan's, where Mr Davenport, the ophthalmic surgeon, would be able to examine Ken before he went on to Battlefield, the officers' house in another part of the village.

When Matron had told Ken about his future movements, she handed him a pocket watch.

"It's a braille watch," she explained.

Ken never knew such things existed, as he flicked open the cover of the smooth hunter at a touch. Sound and touch. Two of the most vital senses left to him. Everyone was presented with a braille watch on entering St Dunstan's, and Ken reacted quite normally. With the cover open, his excited fingers read off the time from its embossed face. The figures were raised, and from the position of the hands he could estimate at once the right time. So, after nearly four months of blindness and asking the time, he could tell it for himself, and St Dunstan's had helped him to take the first small but psychologically important step towards the ultimate aim – independence. Ken never let the watch out of his reach from that first day onward.

After his treatment at Tiger Hall, Ken moved down to Battlefield. It was at this stage that St Dunstan's persuaded Jo that it would be best for them both if she left him and went away for a month or two till he had settled down into the busy atmosphere of the place. They had not been separated since Ken left East Grinstead, but he had to admit the sense in the suggestion and would be bound to benefit later on from the feeling of confidence he hoped to gain from the St Dunstan's training. So, he encouraged Jo to go back to Send.

"We can always phone each other," Ken pointed out.

This would be better and more personal than contact by correspondence, for her letters would have to be read to him, and his dictated to her – in the early stages, at any rate. Both of them thought how public and embarrassing a way this was of communicating between two people so close as they were. For never at any time has Ken's disfigurement lessened Jo's love, only strengthened it. So, she left him to the creative care of St Dunstan's.

A day or so after Jo left, and Ken was still feeling a little lost, Sir (now Lord) Ian Fraser happened to be on one of his frequent visits to Church Stretton with his wife. The then chairman of St Dunstan's made a practice of interviewing and welcoming each new trainee, and Ken's turn came. Sir Ian was, of course, himself blinded as a young second lieutenant in the First World War, and his forceful example has been an inspiration not only to the disabled but to able-bodied men as well. For newly blinded people, particularly, the fact that he has passed the Bar examinations, led St Dunstan's and the British Legion, and at other times held high office with the British Broadcasting Corporation and been a Member of Parliament, must be a spur to success in themselves.

That evening the rest of the officers retired from the dining-room after a glass of port. And over a second glass, Sir Ian and Ken talked of the future, especially Ken's future. Sir Ian did most of the talking, while Ken listened to his exposition of the simple, sane aim of St Dunstan's to fit men once more for full and useful lives.

"The most important thing for anyone with this disability," said Sir Ian, "is to accept it right from the start."

Ken could only have taken such advice from someone such as Fraser who had already proved in his own life the truth of his philosophy. Ken went to bed that night feeling better than he had done since being blinded. He was beginning to see that St Dunstan's looked like doing him good. And the presence of all the other patients in exactly the same state as himself made it much easier.

Some ten blinded officers lived at Battlefield, under the auspices of the matron-hostess, Mrs Irvine, who welcomed Ken into their fold. The St Dunstan's year was divided into three training terms, rather like school, and Ken started his first by sharing a room with a Canadian mining engineer Bill Robinson, and an Englishman, Colin Beaumont-Edmunds. Another 'new boy' like Ken that term was Captain Ernest Halloway. He had been blinded early in the war by a shell from a German raider while on the bridge of his ship, and subsequently taken prisoner. After two and a half years in a P.O.W. camp, Halloway was repatriated at the end of 1943, together with other seriously wounded prisoners. A frequent visitor to the house as Ken joined was Lord Normanby. This wounded officer did a lot while in P.O.W. camp to gather together and commence training the blinded prisoners, and he had been repatriated with the first party of injured, at the same time as Halloway.

The Battlefield scene was not complete to the ten officers without the dry humour – and equally dry opinions – of Walter Mellor. For many years Sir Ian's servant, he had come to Church Stretton 'for the duration' to look after the personal needs of the officers, and to supervise the rest of the staff under Mrs Irvine's direction. They all loved him, and the villagers, too, knew his familiar figure, bowler-hatted on his afternoon off, as he strolled through their midst. One of the genuine original gentleman's gentleman.

Those first few hours settling in at Battlefield gave Ken a chance to pause and look ahead before being launched into the full St Dunstan's course. That was a good sign already. He could look forward to something. He knew that St Dunstan's would regard teaching braille as one of its main contributions towards the process of rehabilitation. In fact, it was really a kind of unwritten condition of entry to the society that the newly blinded St Dunstaner should make a serious attempt to master the mysteries of the embossed code. What Ken did not yet know was the amazing breadth of the training offered at Church Stretton, and that whatever a trainee needed would be made available – however obscure or unusual the subject.

St Dunstan's know about blindness. They are aware that with a disability which cuts people off from all visual appreciation around, loneliness is a constant danger, especially to newcomers. So, they see that there is constant companionship and the succession of images that voices and varied interests produce in the minds of those who poor or no sight. From that original day at Battlefield, Ken had literally no time at all to brood about his problems or his life, until bedtime, and then on that first evening before he could really start to worry, Mrs Irvine gave him other food for thought.

"You'll be starting straight away to-morrow, Mr Revis," she said. "A braille lesson with Lady Buckmaster and a typing lesson with Tommy Rogers."

So, Ken had plenty to think about as he lay in his bed at Battlefield. He had not considered the possibilities of typing. Of course, touch-typing was an obvious asset. He knew of the typical secretarial-school training, but it had hardly occurred to him how it would help him in his present position. And before he fell asleep, he realized that here lay the answer to the embarrassment of dictating letters to Jo. He would learn to type by touch, and then he could correspond freely and privately – even if her letters to him would still have to be read aloud.

Braille and typing were taught quite separately at Longmynd Hotel, which St Dunstan's took over for their stay at Church Stretton. The hotel was up the steep hill beyond Tiger Hall, and V.A.D. guides took the officers there in small groups on the next morning – the Voluntary Aid Detachment was a voluntary unit of civilians providing nursing care for military personnel. Ken and Bill Robinson entered the large lounge of the hotel with their V.A.D. sandwiched between them. The room sounded alive with chatter as the guide directed the pair of them to a settee.

In a few minutes, Lady Buckmaster came up to Ken and claimed him for his first braille lesson. He struggled to his feet from the low settee, to find himself holding a slim, soft hand and listening to the friendly voice of "Lady B," as she was known to every one there. Tucking Ken's hand securely under her arm, she towed him expertly to the braille room.

At that moment, Ken's knowledge of blind people and their ways was still almost non-existent, and he had never encountered any braille before. He half expected to be confronted with some kind of raised characters like those used in printing. But he soon discovered it was different. Conversation all around suggested that they were only two of many in the room. They made themselves comfortable at her special desk. Ken could sense the charm and kindness of Lady B after even so short a time, qualities developed through long experience with the war blinded at St Dunstan's. And for years to come, she was to be closely associated with blind welfare in one way or another.

Lady B handed Ken a small flat box containing several rows of studs, like the tops of round-headed nails. These were much bigger than braille, but helped originally to give beginners the feel of the system, while at the same time growing familiar with the principles on which it is based.

Ken learned that braille was named after the Frenchman, Louis Braille, who devised it over a century ago. Lady B told him how it consisted now as then in reading by touch a series of embossed dots formed rather like the pips on one side of a domino. A braille letter is a minimum of one dot and a maximum of all six, using the various combinations of the arrangement of the dots in this domino form. Each dot is identified by its position down the two rows of three: dot 1, dot 2, dot 3 on the left-hand row; and dot 4, dot 5, dot 6 down the right-hand side.

First of all, Ken had to learn the twenty-six letters of the alphabet. But at this preliminary lesson, Lady B only let him feel the first ten letters, A to J. It was not difficult to distinguish the arrangement of the studs in the box, but, of course, this was not the real braille, merely serving to show the form of the code.

When Lady B gave him some actual braille characters to feel he knew at once that he would be up against a long and formidable task. This was part of the policy for facing facts squarely at St Dunstan's. As Ken moved his fingers over the paper, all he could tell in his depression was that it had some irregular tiny lumps on its surface. He could not make out their shape, number, or arrangement, or, in fact, appreciate that he must be feeling an intelligible series of characters. The large, familiar, friendly nail-heads in their box were one thing; these devilish little dots another. Ken felt furious and at the same time helpless.

"Don't worry – and don't despair," Lady B reassured him. "You'll get to know them in time."

But that night, although he had memorized the arrangements of the letters A to J – and several beyond that – the real braille seemed still to be impossible. Ken could not know that one day he would visit Paris and read the inscription there on the tomb of Louis Braille, built after he had been reinterred and revered almost as a saint. At the moment, Ken's thoughts on the system were far from saintly.

But gradually he began to think of the braille characters as shaped of dots, and they assumed some sort of perspective. There was no short

Ken Revis with his tape-recorder.

The road to Loddon Bridge, near Reading. Loddon Bridge was one of Ken's engineering achievements before the war.

Loddon Bridge completed. A 'tele-snap' by John Cura.

Ken always loved cars. Here is an early effort in the making.

Another early love of Ken's was rugby. Ken is wearing a white sweater and has his arms folded, in the centre of this picture of the Berkshire Wanderers group.

The 1,000-kg Patcham bomb, which was disposed of safely by Ken.

Ken, on the left, being escorted by his best man on the way to his wedding, 1 March 1941.

Jo pictured about the time of her marriage.

The last time that Ken saw Jo – in a garden at Send, Surrey, a few days before the terrible accident.

Brighton's West Pier, where Ken lost his sight when thirteen mines exploded while he was attempting to diffuse them in 1943.

Ken throwing the discuss at the St. Dunstan's sports.

Captain Kenneth Revis, M.B.E., with Jo after receiving his medal from H.M. King George VI.

Three blind men celebrating after the Buckingham Palace investiture at which Ken, seen here on the left, was awarded the M.B.E. Sir Ian Fraser (later Lord Fraser of Lonsdale) is in the centre.

Ken pictured with Sandra, the beautiful white Alsatian guide dog who helped Ken regain his mobility and independence.

Sandra became Ken's "eyes", guiding him safely to and from work each day.

Jane, secretary and sister-in-law, read Ken's law books to him while he was studying.

Ken and Jane on their way to a law lecture in London.

After five years' work, Ken qualifies as a solicitor, and he and Jo celebrate.

Ken on the telephone in his office at the British Motor Corporation.

Ken tried water-skiing.

Ken and Jo revisit the spot where he was blinded on Brighton's West Pier. This was for the B.B.C. television programme *It Happened to Me*.

Shaving the "all-electric way" presented no problems for Ken.

Ken and Jo in the MGA that he drove at 100 m.p.h.

The MGA at speed, with Jo giving steering instructions, but never touching the wheel or other controls.

Ken found flying a glider a stimulating yet restful sport.

Back to earth again! Ken and Jo pictured with his flying instructor.

cut to learning it, and eventually he found himself recognizing odd letters, well-spaced but comforting him quite at random.

Ken got to know the single signs for common combinations of letters such as *gh, sh, th, er, ou.* And then the full-stop. And then the various words which are represented by just one letter of the alphabet written on its own in a sentence. For instance, B means 'but.'

Continuing through the alphabet, Ken came to know that C is 'can,' D is 'do,' E is 'every,' F is 'from,' G is 'go,' H is 'have,' J is 'just,' K is 'knowledge,' L is 'like,' M is 'more,' N is 'not,' P is 'people,' Q. is 'quite,' R is 'rather,' S is 'so,' T is 'the,' U is 'us,' V is 'very,' W is 'will,' X is 'it,' Y is 'you.'

Then there are the separate signs for 'and,' 'for,' 'of,' 'with,' 'mother,' 'father,' and so on.

Since braille is not visual, there is no need for capital letters at the start of a sentence. A full-stop is sufficient to show that a new sentence is about to begin. Nor need the personal pronoun be a capital I. The way that initials are indicated is by writing ordinary letters with full-stops after each of them. So, the British Broadcasting Corporation would be abbreviated to: b.b.c.

Including all word and letter symbols, there are some sixty different combinations of those same six dots to be learned and recognized – quickly. For Ken it was sheer, steady practice. The training also included, of course, using the braille writer. This consists of six keys in a row, for three fingers on each hand, and a space-bar. By pressing the appropriate keys, Ken could write on a braille sheet any of the combinations he was learning.

The uses of braille are many. Two blind people can correspond privately. Someone blind can write it down, and read it back to themselves or anyone else later. And they can read the many publications available in braille. The *National Braille Mail* is a weekly newspaper, and there are other periodicals such as *Braille Radio Times, Readers' Digest, World Digest of Current Fact and Comment, Family Doctor, Intelligence Digest,* and others. These are generally printed by the Royal National Institute for the Blind (the resources available today are, of course, far greater than those available in Ken's time). As Ken progressed, he realized he had to keep it up all the time, or, as in shorthand, he got rusty quickly.

At this early training stage, however, it was mainly a matter of learning: there was no time to forget it yet. Braille music was another mystery yet to be solved by Ken, although he did enter into the St Dunstan's spirit within a week or two by joining an enthusiastic music group there. Two skilled musicians gave instruction. Claude Bampton was an instrumentalist, and John Toner the pianist. With a blind chap on trumpet and Ken at the percussion and tom-tom, they formed a rumba band which was the craze about 1944. Ken started to learn the trumpet, too, and actually brought one away with him when he eventually left St Dunstan's.

The staff and St Dunstaners, in fact, arranged a concert later on at Shrewsbury in aid of the Red Cross, and this Latin-American ensemble played to the fore triumphantly, Ken hitting practically everything within range.

Ken compèred part of the show before the curtain, and also acted in a Colonel Blimp sketch with one of the staff. This private-and-colonel cross-talk went well with Ken as Blimp, until the member of the staff suddenly realized that Ken was moving dangerously near to the footlights at the front of the stage.

"Don't go any farther forward," whispered the private to Ken, "or you'll come a cropper!"

The snag was that Ken could not be sure which way *was* forward. So, he froze instead, and the act went on with the audience unaware of the hissed warning.

Variety is the spice of life. This old slogan had a special significance at St Dunstan's, where the staff knew that they had to try to occupy the patients fully without ever keeping them too long at one thing and risking boring them. So, after braille and music, it was back to typing for Ken with Tommy Rogers. This man had been blinded himself in the First World War, and overcame it as much as anyone could. He gave Ken a series of fifteen lessons, one a day from Monday to Friday for three weeks.

Ken took to typing from the first lesson, and determined to pass the test as soon as it was possible. He concentrated with all his power during these one-hour lessons, with the help of Tommy Rogers and Miss Lloyd. Naturally, however, he had his hurdles to jump here, too, and one day he spent almost the whole hour taking down dictation. He finally rolled the paper out of the machine and held it up for Miss Lloyd to take. She reached Ken, and looked at the sheet he had filled – but there was nothing on it except some impressions that looked more like braille than normal typing. Needless to say, the keys had been on "Stencil," and they had not come in contact with the ribbon at all!

The time he took preparing for the test was considered by Rogers and Miss Lloyd to be just about the shortest on record, and the day came when Ken could actually take the test. Accuracy was the yardstick; speed not necessary. Ken typed the sheet of material dictated to him, trying desperately hard not to make mistakes. Two and a half mistakes were the most allowed, a letter wrong counting as one and punctuation wrong as a half. So, he could really make two errors in letters and one in punctuation. He passed easily, with only one mistake. Each St Dunstaner passing the test was presented with a portable typewriter, and Ken clutched his under his arm after receiving it. Now he could write to Jo without a third person intervening. It was another advance. Slow but sure.

The pattern of Battlefield began to emerge. After the early morning tea Mellor would ask Ken. "What are you going to wear to-day, sir?" Then the valet would lay his suit out, and Ken got down to breakfast about 8.30 a.m.

Some of the officers lived actually at Battlefield, others next door in the annexe. As a constant traffic became inevitable between the two buildings, the staff had cut a hole through the separating hedge and stretched a wire across to indicate a safe walkway for the officers.

The first lesson usually started about 9.30 a.m., and Ken went down to the hotel or to the training centre on the arm of a V.A.D., or possibly the padre, who had a little sight. Two or three of them could travel in one 'convoy.' After an hour's lesson there was a canteen break, and then following the coffee came a further lesson till noon.

On his way back to Battlefield for lunch, Ken got in the habit of going along to the pub for a glass of beer with Captain Halloway, who trusted himself to Ken. The two of them would come out of the training centre and set off down the street. Halloway held on to Ken, and together they practised the route to the pub on the corner. If either had been alone, they would have felt very embarrassed, but as a pair they did not mind at all. Sometimes they felt a stationary car with their sticks as they crossed the road, but they always got round it safely. Halloway was slightly deaf from his injuries as well, so Ken assumed the added responsibility of keeping a keen ear for traffic or other hazards.

Later on, when Jo came up to Battlefield, she would park the car on the other side of the road and watch whether or not they would head for a drink. If she saw them wheel left it meant they would be going straight home for lunch; right, they went for the pub. When it was the latter, she used to wait and give them time to get there and order their drinks, then she strolled across and joined them.

The meals were always served on to their plates, with any meat cut up into easy portions, and Ken found eating reasonably easy, right from the outset. Some blind people had much more difficulty. He got to know how much food he had by the weight of his fork, and could even tell by the balance whether he had a long or short chip!

Life was certainly an adventure. Perhaps that was the way to look at it. Even eating a meal had its hazards and rewards. He slowly started to adopt this fresh attitude. And whereas in his youth he had tended to be slightly superior and aloof at times, now Ken was learning a more tolerant approach.

In the afternoons Ken might have a reader. He listened to books about local government, metallurgy, and cars – still a favourite topic and one he missed most of all. The French and German lessons usually fell in the afternoons, too, and he had an ex-Berlin magistrate for German. Once he and Ken were sitting on the settee in the dining-room at Battlefield, basking in early spring sunshine, when Ken fell asleep as he listened to his teacher reading. The unaccustomed warmth also made the German doctor drowsy, and he nodded off as well. It was only when he actually fell across Ken's lap that they both awoke, feeling distinctly silly.

Early in his training, Ken did a lot of manual work. "Meccano" helped his fingers get nimble without the extra impetus of sight. It also taught him to *remember* things. Where the little box of nuts and bolts was kept, how far he had got with the structure. The lesson of self-sufficiency.

Basket-making he found rather rough on his hands. The points projecting up in the air were also inclined to stick into his face if he was not careful, providing another lesson in memorizing exactly where they were.

They had an upholstery department at Church Stretton, where mattresses and chairs were stuffed very professionally, but Ken concentrated on more mechanical workshops. The first thing he made in the carpentry shop was a letter-rack in the form of a simple stand, followed by a knife box. Slightly more ambitious, Ken shaped a tray that has since seen sixteen summers and shows no sign of wear yet, and is still in the Revis kitchen!

He got to grips with hammers, chisels, saws, nails, and glue. Not to mention gimlets, bradawls, and sandpaper. The only difference in any tools was that the two-foot metal rule had nicks cut out at inch intervals, so that distances could be calculated. Ken did not have any accidents, even slight ones, in the carpentry shop, and all he found was the need for extra care in working. And this working speed naturally seemed slower than when he had sight.

Ken felt most at home, however, in the engineering shop, where he worked a capstan lathe and a router, cutting shapes in aluminium and other metals, and actually making throttle levers for Spitfires. The machinery had the usual industrial safety guards, and Ken soon got to know precisely which part of the equipment was revolving or operating in any other way.

The novelty here was the braille micrometer. The exact dimensions of engineering work is measured on a small sleeve marked in hundredths – even thousandths – of an inch. With the braille version, a thick shank enables embossed readings to be marked and felt around a sleeve as thick as a cocoa tin.

Ken spent a happy month in the engineering shop during his first term at St Dunstan's. They gave him dismantling and reassembly work on an overhead-valve mechanism of a Bristol Pegasus engine. Another job was working a small pump for Ken to develop the idea further of getting used to putting things down, knowing where they are, and keeping nuts and bolts and such-like in special places.

All of this engineering was extremely precise, the router, for instance, being a high-speed machine operating at 24,000 revolutions per minute. And he learned to execute such precision work without ever seeing it. This particular shaping Ken did by working round a template. He pressed down the tool with his foot to draw it up to the metal, and then it cut around the designed shape.

With the approach of the Easter 'holidays' Jo came back to stay at Church Stretton, and Ken began the ordeal of a whole new series of operations on his face. Most of these were done down at Stoke Mandeville, near Aylesbury. For the first one he was taken there by car from Church Stretton, and introduced to Professor Kilner, the plastic surgeon, who would be undertaking the series. To Ken this promised to be an unusual experience, for he had only a local anaesthetic, and so although he would not see anything he remained fully aware of what went on all around him.

Ken was wheeled along the corridor from his ward into the operating theatre, and at once entered a confusing area of voices and sounds. A strange sort of numbness came over the left side of his face – in fact, most of his whole head. The accident and subsequent surgery at East Grinstead had still left vivid red scars sharply marking his left cheek and mouth area. The idea of his first operation was to build up the left cheek, reshape the lower left-eye region, and excise as many of the scars as possible.

Although Ken had only a local anaesthetic, he felt fairly drowsy and was aware of a nurse holding his hand. The surgeon had arrived in gown and gloves, and Ken was aware of the necessary instruments being laid out on a cloth over his chest. Kilner gave clipped instructions all the time, as other operating staff seemed to be putting things down and taking them up regularly.

Kilner was working on the cheek. The sensation to Ken was rather like a visit to the dentist, when the gums have been injected, but the general discomfort remains. Only it was worse. He could actually feel the surgeon at work on his cheek and lower eye.

Ken felt someone holding the nozzle of some bloodsucking device to clean the flow away from near his left eye. Kilner went on talking.

"Suck it away, will you? I want to work there."

And the blood was sucked into the nozzle as Ken's face poured forth. So, the unique experience continued – being conscious yet blind. It seemed to go on for a long time before Kilner was satisfied, and Ken could return to his ward with a sedative. The result, they told him, proved a complete success, Kilner cleverly getting rid of most of the bad scars in the cheek area.

The next one was to knit a large scar between the cheek and mouth. This did not knit quite satisfactorily, however, so another operation had to be scheduled later. These things could never be hurried, of course, for flesh takes its own time to heal, and to try to rush the process is useless. Ken found that as he chewed food, he was tending to bite his lip inside all the time. The cheek-and-mouth knitting had apparently left an inevitable small overhang of flesh within his mouth which would have to be removed. And as Ken smiled, he could still only lift the right-hand side of his mouth and face. Beyond the scar between his nose and mouth on the left he had little feeling either in his face or the gums. This operation turned out to be another awkward one, as the excess flesh was cut out from his mouth and a row of stitches inserted all along the inside of it. For a long time after these stitches had healed, Ken received massage on his left lip, and then subsequently he had orders to carry on with the treatment himself. Every day he massaged upward, gradually getting more mobility in his mouth and adjacent parts.

So, they came on to the nose itself. Some reshaping could be accomplished outside, but most of it had to be done internally. For the S.M.R. – sub-mucous rectomy – Ken was told he would have local anaesthetics. He wondered what to expect this time, although he knew that the theory was to cut away the bone at the back of the nose – not the pleasantest prospect even under a general anaesthetic.

It was the same story of the ride to the operating theatre, and despite it all Ken stuck to his strong opinion which he gave to a friend.

"I rather enjoy the ops. Quite frankly, they're a change from routine, and I know I'm being well looked after all the time."

The purpose of removing some of this bone at the back of the nose was partly to ease his nasal breathing, partly for reshaping. In other words, half practical, half aesthetic.

By the time Ken had got settled on the operating table, Kilner was chatting away as usual and the whole scene seemed familiar, almost as if Ken were really seeing it.

"Now we've got to bind up your head," he heard Kilner saying.

And at that, they began to roll several thicknesses of solid binding around his forehead as tightly as they could. It seemed to be done with all someone's strength, and felt very constricting. Then they directed his head between twin wedges, so that he could not move it either way. As before, the instruments appeared to be laid out on top of Ken. And like previous operations, too, Ken had taken out his eyes in the ward, as he did each night, keeping them in a small receptacle.

The first shock came when they injected an anaesthetizing needle right up his nose, and then into his cheek. Both these injections had to be on the left side, the half of his face still so tender, and they were extremely painful.

With Ken's head securely wedged in place, Kilner took a delicate surgical chisel, pushed it up Ken's nostril, and hit it with a hammer. Despite the anaesthetic, the noise and shock to the system felt acute. His head was being punched, clouted, back into the wedges, and he could do nothing about it. Like being pinned flat in a dentist's chair.

"Are you all right?" Kilner asked.

"Yes," Ken managed to gasp.

He heard the hollow clangs in his head like the hours being struck by Big Ben, His whole nervous system seemed on edge, shattered, as it awaited the next hit. Kilner had to go on striking and chipping away. Minutes went by. Each hammer blow felt as if an hour had passed and struck. All Ken's reaction concentrated into the single overwhelming sense of sound. Suddenly it was all over, and he was being wheeled back to the ward, with the strikes still echoing in his dazed brain. Then a sedative and sleep. So much for S.M.R.

Ken's features were at last pronounced ready for the operation to give him his first more or less complete nose since the previous September. What remained of his real one was still badly battered and flattened into the face. This important operation became due during 'term time,' so Ken had it at Church Stretton. Although Tiger Hall was the St Dunstan's hospital, operation cases went to the Longmynd Hotel, so Ken found himself flat on a stretcher again and riding in an ambulance to the hotel. Kilner operated, inserting a tantalum bridge into his nose. This lustrous white metal looked like silver, and it was the first time it had ever been used as a bridge in plastic surgery. Kilner told Ken afterwards that he was well pleased with the results, and he had had fun forming the tantalum into a ridge like the roof of a house.

Ken was out and about again fairly soon, and one of the first things was for him to be hurrying along the village road, almost blasé by now, when he walked right into the back of a stationary bus with his precious new nose! The only excuse he could offer was that he was hurrying to meet Jo, who lived within easy reach of St Dunstan's.

So, a strange summer came around. The seasons would go on, whether Ken saw them or not. He did feel the warmth, however, and smelt the summer scents. Luckily, he was discovering by now that this year at St Dunstan's – despite the operations – was certainly the best thing that could happen to a blinded person. The only possible time for depression came when he was alone in bed at night, but now even that did not seem so bad with Jo only a mile or so off. Then life soon started up again with the early morning tea.

There was always something to look forward to each week. Ken made a quick recovery from his operations, and started practising for the St Dunstan's sports. On the great day, he went in for the half-mile walk, with the aid of a guide who held on to him with a ribbon just to see he went in the right direction.

Gradually during sports practices, too, Ken got used to running blind. This calls for complete confidence, but it came in time for the actual day. The 100-yards event was organized by timing each competitor with a stop-watch. Instead of sight, they used sound, and ran towards a ringing bell which was located at the end of the distance from the starting-point.

Ken entered for everything he could, including the standing long jump. As they could not attempt the normal running long jump, the aim of this event was to leap as far as possible from a static position. To throw the discus and for putting the shot, Ken had to feel with his foot for a piece of rod, which indicated the thro wing-point. Luckily no one hurled any offensive weapons towards the spectators!

Ken and an R.A.F. officer were the only two commissioned men to take part in the sports. During one of the afternoon's events, one of the other St Dunstaners said to Ken, "You know, some of you officers aren't bad chaps at all!"

Ken was quick to reply, "And some of you aren't bad chaps at all either!"

One last sports item involving Ken was the tug-o'-war. The teams used to pull in shirts, shorts, and Army boots, and after the event on sports day, a few of the other ranks invited him up to their house for supper, which he felt pleased to accept. As far as he was concerned, the war was over and they were all the same now. One or two of the officers, however, did seem to preserve that gulf between themselves and the men.

Ken became so proficient that he was the only officer in the St Dunstan's tug-o'-war team, which also served to bring him closer to the men. Once they went to the local barracks at Shrewsbury to pull against the Army team there. Ken heaved with all his heart, and the St Dunstan's team held the Army for nearly four minutes before being beaten.

Ken had always been very fit physically, but these activities were really remarkable in view of the injuries he had suffered the previous autumn, and all the operations since then.

So already he was living much more fully than he thought conceivable when he joined St Dunstan's. But more still remained to be achieved there – and afterwards.

St Dunstan's used to run dances in a little hall next to the canteen, and Ken turned up regularly at these as he knew he could cope with any problems involved after his experience with Jo at the New Year's dance a few months earlier. The St Dunstaners actually included a small number of blinded women, who were in demand as partners, while guests could also be brought to the dances. Normally the girls who were blind danced with partners who had their sight, and the men found female staffer guests to guide them. The only difference really was that the sighted partner kept a little more on the look-out.

Ken perfected his bump of direction by sound, and so could pinpoint the band and thus the rest of the hall. Jo partnered him at one or two of these dances, and she was astonished here as elsewhere at the precision he had acquired in locating people and places solely by sound. As far as the actual dancing went, Ken was as good as ever, and still found some partners more awkward than others!

The summer brought tandem rides through the leafy Shropshire lanes, with Ken riding behind one of the staff. Country walks, too, brought the sweet scents of summer to Ken's partly restored nose. They would set off with two St Dunstaners on each arm of a V.A.D. guide, presenting a row of five marching along the winding paths. Often a couple of V.A.D.s led four each for a long walk, making a total of ten. They took a picnic when the weather was good enough, or else aimed for some special place for tea. Or perhaps a pub might be the goal if one lay on a convenient route. The V.A.D. girls were all extremely nice, and had taken up this as war work.

So, the round continued, with an occasional party arranged as something special to look forward to in life. The whole course appeared almost casual, but in fact it was worked out with deep understanding of the men and women at Church Stretton. Men like Ken, who was already on the way towards overcoming his disability.

Ken had ridden a horse a bit in the past, but never regularly. When one of the V.A.D.s offered to take him out riding, he jumped at the chance. It was something different, and one more thing he had not thought of doing. In theory, a blind person can go out riding alone, but it is better to be accompanied, as there are always obstacles like overhanging branches and half-shut gates in the way. Ken found that the girl's voice helped his direction, and altogether the rides went very well, down quiet lanes and over open country.

One day they were trotting along a lane quietly when Ken's horse was suddenly startled, and shied up steeply. Bucking a second time, the animal pitched Ken right over his head. Not knowing what was happening, nor what might come next, Ken could not control the horse or himself, and made a three-point landing on the verge of the lane, with nothing worse than a bruise to add to his other scars. Ken did not like the feeling of being thrown through the air and being unable to do anything about it except grope out with his hands.

Jo went riding with him another time. They were on a really narrow path and Ken had taken the lead on his horse, when Jo's bolted as she came through a little gate. Ken sensed that something was wrong, and thought quickly as the hooves grew louder. With a wrench on the reins, he turned his horse round sideways and blocked the complete path. Then he had only a second to wait before Jo came blundering into him. The collision calmed the animal down, and no harm came to either of them.

One thing Ken gradually discovered during this year was that a blind person cannot really relax. Normal people can take it easy and 'tick over' every so often, but those with poor or no sight stop altogether if they do the same. For them every single action is a strain on some sense, and to keep level with life they are continually geared up. So much that comes instinctively to those with sight needs positive physical and mental exertion by people like Ken.

Meanwhile this year of their strange new life went on for Ken and Jo. He persuaded Jo to come for a tandem ride, which attracted considerable attention from the villagers as they set off. Jo had to take the front seat of the male tandem, and by the time she negotiated the cross-bar and they pushed off from the kerb, the tandem was launched on a perilous zigzag towards the Church Stretton traffic-lights! They swerved and nearly sprawled over, before finally getting the hang of the balance and setting a steady, rhythmic pace. As usual, Ken was doing his bit, but it had to be up to Jo to steer him.

The house called The Yeld, where Jo stayed that summer and autumn, stood on the outskirts of the village, and belonged to a lady with five children of ages ranging from about ten into the twenties. Their ponies grazed in the grounds, and it was generally an ideal country house. Ken came up there to dinner sometimes, and with familiarity the house became known to them as The Yell.

Jo returned the visits by reading to some of the officers at Battlefield, and helping them to do crossword puzzles. The anniversary of Ken's accident passed, and it scarcely seemed possible to them that they had lived a year since the ghastly day the previous September. And soon after this they were invited to Buckingham Palace for the investiture of Ken's M.B.E. – Member of the Most Excellent Order of the British Empire.

They decided to make it an occasion to remember, and so stayed at the Savoy for a few days that week. Jo drove them down from Church Stretton, and they reached London the afternoon before the investiture. The trees lining the Embankment were shedding their leaves, and they glimpsed the Thames through the blacked-out dusk.

For Ken's birthday, soon after his accident, Jo's father had bought him an electric razor which he had used every day since. Ken got it out next morning and plugged it into the socket – only to find it was the wrong voltage and would not work. They had to be at the Palace quite early, so a frantic call went out for the barber in the Savoy who could make him look presentable for the occasion. Ken got his shave safely, but the barber had a hard job using a normal razor on Ken's facial injuries. The next panic came as Jo hurried down the Savoy stairs in a pair of new high-heeled shoes. She was not yet used to them, and twisted her ankle slightly four or five steps from the bottom. She slithered the rest of the way and half fell over right into the arms of Rex Harrison, who happened to be there at that moment!

"Do you usually come downstairs like that?" he asked as he helped her up again.

Ken's mother was allowed into the Palace with them, and the St Dunstan's Press officer met the three of them inside. They were ushered into an enormous hall, where a Court official asked Ken to accompany him. Ken felt himself sitting on a high-backed padded chair without arms. He heard the noise of the room in front of him and the echo of it behind, so knew that the chair was up against a wall. Another official meanwhile asked Jo in a booming voice to go with him, explaining that they would like her to meet Ken at the foot of a carpeted slope after the King had decorated him.

97

Ken heard someone else being shown to a seat alongside, so leaned across to introduce himself and ask the other man's name. He turned out to be another St Dunstaner, Jimmy Wright, an R.A.F. pilot who had been badly scarred in an air crash. Then a third blind man sat beside them. He was a Methodist Army Chaplain who had been blinded in a grenade accident, and the three of them sat and whispered between the burly forms of a couple of beefeaters. Their little group was at the foot of the steps on one side of the dais, while Jo and the two next of kin of the other blinded men made a similar trio down the other side, having a perfect view of the dais itself.

When the moment for Ken finally arrived, he was shown up the slope and told to turn left and bow to King George VI, who asked him how he had been blinded. Ken gave him the brief details of the Brighton Pier episode.

"And how long have you been at St Dunstan's?" the King asked.

"About nine months, Your Majesty." "I hope they're looking after you well and that you're getting on well there and feeling happy." "Yes, thank you, sir." "Very well done."

The King pinned the M.B.E. medal on Ken, shook hands with him, and it was all over. Ken turned right, and his guide took his elbow and led him away, signalling to Jo to come and meet him. Together they walked the length of the hall to an official, who packaged the medal and handed it back to Ken in its box. Mrs Revis was waiting for them both, and in a few minutes they were in a taxi down the Mall, heading for the Savoy and a special celebration lunch-party. Ken and Jo have never forgotten that lunch given by Sir Ian and Lady Irene "Chips" Fraser. The guests of honour were, of course, Ken and the Methodist Minister, but as well as Sir Ian and Lady Fraser, Jo and Mrs Revis, and the Reverend's relations, the party included Sir Archibald McIndoe from East Grinstead, Raymond Quilter, Ken's old Bomb Disposal friend and an enthusiastic expert on cars, and Colonel Marshall, of Bomb Disposal.

Ken met Sir Ian again soon after the luncheon when the Chairman made one of his regular visits to Church Stretton. Sir Ian knew that Ken was nearing the end of his year there, and wanted a chat with him to discuss his future.

Sir Ian was obviously pleased with Ken's progress. "When you finish your year," he said, "I can offer you one of two jobs." Ken listened intently, wondering what to expect. "One would be to understudy the industrial-settlements officer of St Dunstan's, if that appeals to you." But before Ken could consider whether or not he would like it, the Chairman went on, "The other job is to go out East and help run the Indian St Dunstan's." Ken wondered if he had heard rightly.

"I'd like to go to India very much, sir. I ought to ask my wife before I decide, so can I let you know definitely to-morrow?"

They exchanged brief notes on what the job would entail in India, developing the service for the increasing number of war blinded out there, and then Ken asked if he could go and tell Jo all about it. He felt so strongly in favour of the idea that he found his way alone all the way from Battlefield, through the village, and right to The Yeld. Here was something to be done, a definite job, and a useful one, too. He knew instinctively that Jo would feel the same. Sure enough, Jo jumped at the new prospect, with all her tremendous zest for fresh experience, and Ken duly confirmed his decision next day.

During those final few weeks at Church Stretton, Ken represented St Dunstan's officially for the first time. A town in Lincolnshire had collected a sum for St Dunstan's, and they asked if someone could visit there to accept the cheque on its behalf. Jo drove Ken over to her home county, and he made a short speech of thanks for the cheque. By now as well Ken was digesting everything he could find about India. Jo and other volunteers read an enormous tome to him, a gazetteer of India, and they left Battlefield feeling slightly more familiar with the country. The more practical side of the studies would take nine or ten months, however, so they would not be leaving for a long time yet.

After another Christmas home at Sleaford, more cheerful than the last one, they piled all they possessed into the obliging car once more and set the bonnet south for London to learn the complete job of blind welfare. On the way they called at an Indian Army camp at Thetford, in Cambridgeshire, to talk to some of the Indian officers who were in training there.

Their home for 1945 was to be the Overseas Club, St James, just round the corner from the Ritz, and although the year meant a lot of work and travelling, they also enjoyed a whirl of social and theatre life in London.

The secretary of St Dunstan's outlined the plan for Ken to go around all St Dunstan's departments and also those of the National Institute for the Blind. Part of the duties during this period was also to understudy Sir Ian and Lady Fraser at various functions, following the principle of having a blind person to represent St Dunstan's.

The days were never long enough at this time. Both Ken and Jo were enrolled for work once or twice a week at the School of Oriental and African Studies, a department of the London University. Here they had individual tuition from the author of a textbook on colloquial Urdu, and this was specially brailled for Ken into two volumes by the National Institute for the Blind. They had to translate all the Indian sounds into an acceptable code for comprehension, and Ken had to learn fifteen or twenty of these special sounds. The whole job of learning this basic Urdu was extremely tedious, with the extra effort of remembering the Indian sounds, but before he had finished, he could carry on a simple conversation in the language.

The Indian teacher was horrified one day when Jo was trying to convey to Ken a particular character.

"It's like the mark left by sparrows' feet that have hopped in the snow!" An unorthodox comparison, but Ken got the idea all right.

This was really a time of rediscovering life for them both. Ken loved to explore the club by himself. There were some minor mishaps, however, when he would try to use the swing doors alone! Once or twice, he pushed people's faces in as they entered and he was searching for the doors to leave the club! And there were also a few cases of heels and toes hit by doors as he swung them around in ignorance of anyone using them at the time!

A sense of humour was essential, they both found, as they often became the centre of attention. Sometimes people's interest reached the stage of rudeness. Some Polish officers sat next to Ken and Jo at the club for meals for several days, and used to watch fascinated while Jo cut up any awkward food for Ken. After they had been staring for about three days, Jo got a bit fed up and called across to them, pointing at Ken's plate, "Old English custom, you know."

They were beginning to find out how strangely some people treat those who had no sight. When Ken and Jo went to a restaurant for a meal more than once this year a waiter or waitress would speak only to Jo.

"Does he take sugar in his coffee?" one waiter whispered to her.

"Yes, I jolly well do!" Ken roared. "I may be blind, but I'm not deaf and dumb and daft, too!" he added to Jo.

About eighteen months after the accident, Ken got his second pair of plastic eyes. Originally, he had mere shells inserted to stop the sockets shrinking, and then that first plastic pair. These had proved useful, but he knew that they were not ideal and often felt a bit embarrassed, being aware of their inadequacy. So, Ken always had it in mind to get rid of them as soon as he could, and when early in 1945 it was agreed that the eye-sockets had found their final shape he arranged for an appointment with the R.A.F. dental department at Uxbridge.

Jo drove him down there from the club, and they met Squadron Leader Stewart, an expert at making these still-new acrylic resin eyes. Stewart directed Ken into an ordinary dentist's chair, put his head back, and poured a warm pinkish colloidal substance right into each eye-socket to take an impression not only of the shape of the socket but of every muscle as well. Ken can move artificial eyes because these muscles at the back are still functioning perfectly well. Stewart left this waxy impression in each socket for about half an hour to set, and as far as Ken was concerned the first visit was at an end, except for replacing his old eyes.

When he returned to Uxbridge next his new eyes had been made in the dental surgery there, but before he felt them in his sockets Stewart had to take various measurements and sightings from every angle. While Ken waited anxiously, the squadron leader was making one or two preliminary adjustments to these eyes with a 'ripply' shape at the back. Finally, he told Ken, "Here you are; you can put them in now. Move the lids about and get them as comfortable as you can."

Ken popped them in, but felt a bit of pressure here and there which hurt him. Stewart grunted, and then ground pieces off each eye with meticulous care. Then they went in again. This happened once or twice before Stewart was satisfied they were as near perfect as he could hope.

The next job was to colour them to match Ken's original deep-blue shade. With Jo's expert help, they achieved a good likeness, and the actual appearance of the eyes was remarkably natural. The East Grinstead pair had been too strongly coloured, giving rather a staring countenance, which Ken was glad to lose.

The new pair felt distinctly different for a while, which was only to be expected, but they were certainly much better moulded. The old ones had a more pointed, chestnut-shaped look, and they did not fit so well as these new eyes as soon as Ken got used to them.

Ken continued to avoid the wind or other drying influence, for if it dried the surface film over the eyes it left a certain soreness. So long as he kept out of high winds or open cars, he found little trouble, and the natural moisture in the ducts allowed the eyes to remain well lubricated. Another phenomenon he noticed was that when he got particularly worried over anything, it reacted by creating soreness in his eyes. Meanwhile he bathed his eyes occasionally, and gradually got accustomed to them. The main thing was always if the eye dried and then he blinked, then it would rub and be painful.

After a while he found that the eyes were inclined to become very slightly rough, but with a little trial and error they soon discovered that all they need do was clean them every three months or so with ordinary metal polish! Of course, Ken still took them out at night, and bathed his sockets and the eyes with warm water.

Even in 1945, he was one of the earliest blinded persons to have plastic eyes, and this pair proved so good that Ken decided he ought to have a spare set made in case anything happened to them far away in India. This second pair were identical to the first, except for a slight difference in colouring which only Jo could distinguish.

When with Stewart, being measured for the second pair, Ken said to him, "I'll have to get a bloodshot pair as well for Sunday-morning hangovers!"

He guarded his eyes more than anything else, almost as if they were real. If he went into a strange wash-room, at a hotel or a friend's house, and removed them, he had to make sure first that the plug was securely in the hole of the basin, so that they could not fall through if they rolled off the ledge.

So, Ken felt he could face the world better now with a pair of plastic eyes that looked really natural, even to slight movement. In fact, he has fooled people subsequently about them several times. Once, when he was staying in London on his own, his foot started to swell so that he could not stand. There was nothing to be done but go to bed and call a doctor, who duly arrived and sat down at his bedside. The first question was not about Ken's foot, but the inevitable one.

"Do you want to be treated privately or as a National Health patient?"

Ken did not want to pay, and told him so.

"All right. Sign this form, will you?"

"Where?" Ken asked.

"Where it says."

"Well, I'll sign it if you'll show me where – I'm blind, you see."

"Good God. I had no idea!"

The doctor was only a yard away from Ken, and, needless to say, his tone softened noticeably from then on. After he left the room, Ken sat up in bed chuckling to himself; he had fooled his first doctor.

Ken and Jo were taken to every part of the two organizations. They found that St Dunstan's were much better off and luckier than the National Institute for the Blind, which had to look after more people with less money.

They started by being shown all the various supplies then available for blind welfare. The braille watches and writing machines Ken already knew well, and now he went into the mysteries of the then latest idea – talking books. St Dunstan's had their own talking-book research department, which kept abreast of the current advances in these twelve-inch long-playing records. These were well established as early as 1945, several years before commercial L.P.s came on to the market for music, and the technique was to record whole books read by experienced B.B.C. men. With their forthcoming trip to India always in mind, Ken read his first talking book – *The Rains Came* by

102

Louis Bromfield. The descriptive passages he found very interesting, even if the story itself happened to be a bit more lurid than likely to be met. But talking books were a great idea which could be invaluable to St Dunstan's in India just as over here.

Ken and Jo got an overall impression of the whole scope of work for those who were blind, some exciting, some more prosaic yet equally important. He had some time with the pensions officer, for instance, to learn how to smooth out men's problems of payment and so avoid more hardship than the disabled already had to endure. It is absolutely essential that those who were blind should not have to worry about money and their dependants, but to concentrate on the problem of learning to live to the best possible purpose. He discussed general problems with the welfare officer of St Dunstan's, who handled other ranks while the Frasers coped with officers' welfare.

Everything possible is done by St Dunstan's, even down to designing gadgets for individual needs. One man about that time had lost his hands as well as being blinded, so the St Dunstan's experimental officer adapted a change machine – rather like the London Underground type – so that he could partly run a tobacconist's shop on his own. The coins slid down a ramp towards him, and he was also able to give change to the customers automatically.

The shops department of St Dunstan's, incidentally, often buys premises and lets them to the member. Similarly, the estates department helps members buy houses by surveying them and arranging mortgages when the property is satisfactory. This particular department has been run for some time by Peter Matthews, who, like Ken, was formerly in Bomb Disposal. Matthews used to be an estate agent before the War, so this work is ideal for him.

Among all this travelling, Ken and Jo managed to maintain an average of two visits a week to London theatres. They liked both straight plays and musicals, and Ken could appreciate the performances perfectly well. Contrary to some people's belief, a blind person does not necessarily become half-witted as well. Jo's scheme when theatre-going, which she has always followed since then, was to arrive ten minutes or more before the start and read the programme to Ken. This gave him an idea of the time and place of the play and also of the cast. Then, as soon as the curtain rose, she whispered a concise description of the actual set to him, with details of where the doors, stairs, furniture, and windows were, and also the style of the setting. If the scene changed for Act II, she repeated this. Apart from occasional comments, called for when something entirely visual was in progress, she did not have to help him anymore. So, the theatre was just one more activity which Ken could enjoy almost as much as if he still had his sight. They were pursuing the policy of St Dunstan's that a full life is a happy one – and leaves less time to worry.

Ironically, Ken returned to Brighton, too, visiting the St Dunstan's training centre and convalescent home at Ovingdean. He met the matron and many others there, and heard how it was run. From there it was back to London to discuss the *St Dunstan's Review* with its editor. Then the all-important question of settlement in industry. Ken visited various homes and factories to see how blind people and employers were feeling about taking on the disabled. There was legislation to insist on this, of course, but it was always better for things to be done voluntarily. When Ken explained the sort of work that those who were blind could do, he frequently found firms more amenable to consider employing them. And in this respect, he himself acted as a good example to employers. Too many people were – and still are – inclined either to write off the visually impaired as useless or else consider them only as fit for compassion. When, like other disabled persons, all they want is a chance to fit into the fabric of life and show what they can do.

While near Birmingham on a visit, Ken and Jo met the man who was later to become the operational head of Bomb Disposal and an almost legendary figure in post-War work – Major A.B. ("Bill") Hartley. Like Ken, Hartley was awarded the M.B.E. for his work on beach mines, and he later followed it up with a George Medal to crown a career of courage.

For the life ahead of Ken courage of a different kind was needed, and day by day he was revealing that he would not be lacking. Jo could see how the accident and its aftermath had definitely strengthened Ken's character still further.

And still in the Midlands, the two of them went to the heart of training for those who were blind, to a school where children were being taught from the age of four or five up to School Certificate standard and even beyond to the universities. The curriculum had to cope with such visual problems as how to explain the theories of geometry to someone without sight. Ken came away from this place with the sound of the children's voices echoing in his head and feeling a real sense of humility.

The communication of knowledge and information is a prime part of blind welfare, and Ken and Jo became absorbed in the printing processes of the braille publications at the National Institute for the Blind. They were amazed at the ingenious way braille was printed on an aluminium master-plate and then pressed out by the thousand. Everything from knitting patterns to popular songs. Even advertisements for "Lifebuoy," "Chilprufe," and the latest books.

Back to Brighton again one day to see an offshoot of the standard system of printing for those who were blind. This is the less-known Moon system, invented by a man of that name in the nineteenth century, rather later than braille. This is a type of embossed figuring simpler than braille and used mainly for elderly people who find the standard system too much for them. It has larger characters that are easier to the touch than braille, and Ken and Jo waited while a paper was being printed there. It came on strings, shaking as it went along on a drying machine till it emerged as a rather more spongy product than braille. But Moon had to be seriously considered, especially as Ken and Jo would be going to a part of the world less advanced generally than in Britain.

Ken's work in India would be to assist the blinded Sir Clutha Mackenzie at St Dunstan's out there, and also help him in his capacity as advisor to the Indian Government on blind welfare. With the war not yet over in the East, it was thought that to undertake such work Ken should be recommissioned in the Army. It was further decided that he would be offered the rank of captain in the Indian Army. As the date of 1 August 1945, had been suggested as suitable for joining, Ken and Jo made one or two trips to Hawkes of Savile Row for his uniform and general tropical equipment. Normally they were extremely careful in shops to avoid the chance of damage, but on one of these visits to the exclusive Service tailors Ken unfortunately hooked his guiding stick around one of the fully laden series of glass shelves, supporting uniforms and dummies and other gear. The quiet of Savile Row was shattered by the crash of glass as everything on the shelves collapsed all over the floor. Ken could only stand and listen to the chaos around him. A brigadier popped his head out of a fitting-room, and most occupants of the other cubicles looked to see what had happened. Ken and Jo apologized abysmally, but the management were wonderful and brushed aside any embarrassment, telling them that it was "quite all right."

So, on 1 August Ken presented himself at India House for an informal recommissioning, becoming a rare, if not unique, case of a blind Army officer. The only other one Ken knew was Sir Ian Fraser, commissioned as a lieutenant-colonel during the War. Now Ken was nearly ready for the East with his light tropical kit. As long as he wore the Indian Army cap-badge they raised no objection to his keeping the Royal Engineers emblems and sapper buttons. He rounded off the uniform with a khaki beret. These had only just come into service at the time of Ken's accident, so he hardly remembered ever seeing one.

After the summer leave, they started the last lap of their preparations, and by about October they were really packing in earnest. St Dunstan's allowed them the use of a whole basement beneath the London offices, where Ken and Jo soon filled two wardrobe trunks with clothes and as many of their personal household things as they could. Ken also packed some talking books, a braille writer, braille literature, and one or two pocket frames for writing braille. These ingenious frames consisted of two flat pieces of aluminium the approximate size of a postcard. A piece of paper was placed between the aluminium sheets, and to the accompaniment of popping noises it was possible to make brief braille notes by hand. When all the Revis baggage eventually saw the light of day before being loaded on board ship, it was found to weigh in the vicinity of one ton, compared to the four hundredweights they had been officially allowed to take!

They made the round of their parental homes in farewell, and received another lunch from the Frasers, at Claridges this time. Ken and Jo got on well with them. Ken was not afraid to stand up to the force of the man's personality, while both of them liked "Chips" Fraser enormously. She could deal with anyone at all levels of society, and then as always was the perfect support for Sir Ian, to whom she has devoted her life. He often used a braille frame so that he could refer to notes when making a speech. A remarkable man who determined to succeed despite his disabilities.

Ken and Jo had the surprise of being seen off at Liverpool by Captain Halloway and his wife. Halloway was the merchant skipper who had arrived at St Dunstan's on the same day as Ken. They waved the voyagers off, and as the Swedish ship *Drottningholm* slipped into the murky Mersey fog, to Ken and Jo it was as if they had stepped into another world.

Chapter 8

INDIAN INTERLUDE

After six years of war, the ship seemed the essence of luxury, with
everything clean, every one courteous, and the food unrationed. There
were about 500 second-class passengers and 150 first class. Ken and
Jo went first, and found that most of their companions were women
going to join husbands in the East. Ken – now Captain Kenneth Revis,
M.B.E., Indian Army – and a major and another captain were the only
three men in uniform, so their parties found themselves at the same
dining table, soon nicknamed "the Army council" by other passengers.
The captain was on his way to Port Said en route to join the Arab
Legion. The Mediterranean lay ahead. They had the prospect of a
perfect voyage.

Ken made his usual point of studying the geography of his
surroundings, so that he could get about on his own whenever possible
or necessary. The bathroom was quite near, and he could comfortably
feel his way along there. Then there were the various passageways near
their cabin and the glass-enclosed deck, where they could sit and relax.
Sometimes he went down to breakfast before Jo, and to other meals
occasionally apart from her, finding his way down one of two winding
staircases that twisted till they finally joined in the dining saloon. Then,
unless a steward spotted him, he plodded across to the Army council
table. Jo deliberately encouraged this sense of independence as often as
she felt Ken wanted it. She was learning the tricky art of looking after
him without appearing to him to be doing so.

In the Bay of Biscay, the weather lived up to its reputation, and many
of the passengers could scarcely keep upright on the rolling decks.
Through it all, Ken walked round quite at ease and perfectly balanced.

The only mishap he had was when he knocked a little Swede down a
narrow companionway. When the Scandinavian saw that Ken was blind
all he replied to the profuse apologies was, "Yes, please, thank you!"

Once in the Mediterranean the Army council table and others adjacent really took over the serious business of entertainment aboard. Ken and Jo were elected to the ship's committee for the purpose, and in no time at all a whole series of activities had been started. Jo has always been crazy about the theatre and entertainment of all kinds, so felt right in her element. For the treasure hunt, Ken composed all the clues in the form of rhyming couplets which directed the competitors from the wireless cabin to the bar, and on to all points of the vessel.

He competed in the sucking-the-milk-fastest contest. Jo had to feed him with a giant bottle of tasteless powdered milk thrust into his mouth, and excitement grew as the level of the liquid shrank in each bottle. Eventually Ken sucked his last drop only a second or two after the winner, and was rewarded with the second prize of a bottle, not of milk, but of champagne.

They made acquaintance with 'milk' of another kind soon after this. When a Swedish friend first asked them to have a mid-morning drink, they were just wondering what to have when he suggested, "How about cocoa?"

"Well . . . . "

"I will arrange it."

The Swede disappeared, and then returned with a steward and some glasses of brown, milky-looking liquid which turned out to be a cocoa liqueur containing brandy, and otherwise known as Tiger's Milk. It certainly seemed as strong as that animal!

So, the days passed in a succession of parties, sweepstakes, fancy-dress dances, and all the other frivolities of an ocean trip so remote from the recent war.

Ken decided that the male passengers needed a bit of proper exercise, so organized a tug-o'-war between the first and second classes. They set the day a little ahead to give both teams time to train, but Ken found the first-class men "far from that condition." In fact, as he could not get them away from the bar to train, he had to make them practise proper grips on the rail of the bar between drinks! When the appointed time arrived, and the two teams lined up at opposite ends of the ship's rope, the sturdier second-class men outpulled them completely, despite Ken's own efforts. Every one enjoyed this interlude in the Indian Ocean.

Near the end of that long last leg across the shimmering sea, Ken was given a handsome pipe by an Indian he had met on board. So on to Bombay and the huge Johnny Walker whisky sign, one of the first sights from the harbour. To Ken the impressions were different as the ship edged alongside. Heat, strange smells, the sounds of running coolies, baggage being moved, the hubbub of Hindustani voices, and, above this, the intermittent berthing orders. It all conveyed to him a merging blur of movement, excitement, colour.

Ken and Jo had got to know two charming people on board, David David and his sister, Mrs Florence Shepherd. Pamela Aitken, wife of a Bombay solicitor, who met them all in her large American car, whisked them off for a midday drink and lunch at the Yacht Club. Ken and Jo both felt pretty thirsty in the heat, and accepted the suggestion of pomegranate juice.

The entire essence of India was contained for Ken in that enormous pint-size of pure pomegranate juice. He could see it shining pink with sunlight in the glistening glass, and could taste its exotic flavour. We've really arrived, he thought.

The Frontier Mail rattled its route northward through a thousand miles of dusty, inscrutable, interior India. At the endless succession of small stations, Jo saw scrawny arms plunged into their carriage, and Ken heard the assortment of voices in broken English.

"You want to buy something, sahib?"

No bedding was provided in the Indian sleeping-berths, so they were very glad of their Jaeger sleeping-bags on the first night, which seemed as if it would never end. At last, they were north of the Tropic of Cancer and heading for the Delhi area. By the next night the train climbed high among the hill country, with its passes through the mountains. The tunnels cut in the hills were icy. Now that they were approaching the end of the 36-hour journey, they had to be sure that they got out at the right station, but in the velvety Indian night Jo could scarcely see anything. Each time the train stopped, therefore, whether at a station or not, they both poked their heads out of the window and called to anyone who might be there:

"Saharanpur?"

They heard half a dozen "No's" before finally finding themselves there about 2 a.m. This was certainly a new experience; arriving at a remote railway station in the middle of the night, not far from the Himalayas, though to Ken the dark seemed no different from day – only colder.

Sir Clutha Mackenzie met them, but the trip was not yet over. A two-hour car-ride lay between Saharanpur and their destination, Dehra Dun, location of the Indian St Dunstan's. Just before dawn the car approached what was to be their bungalow. Ken recognized the house by the crunch of the gravel drive under the wheels. Then he sensed himself beneath a portico by the slight echo and enclosed feeling.

"Salaam, sahib," the servant on duty greeted them.

Sir Clutha suggested a rest after their long trek, adding, "I've got a good bearer for you called Abdul. He'll look after you well." When they reached their room, they dropped into bed for six or seven hours.

The next Ken knew was a voice saying, "I'm Abdul, sahib."

From that first meeting Jo could see that the Indian adored Ken, and in no time, he had got to know all their needs. She used to take a bath and dress first in the mornings, followed by Ken. When he stepped into the galvanized iron bath, guided by Abdul, Ken had the soap handed to him, and then the towel afterwards. His slippers were in the precise place by the bath. Abdul was waiting to dress him, although Ken did not really approve. Every time Ken came home to the big bungalow, the bearer insisted on cleaning his dusty shoes, and at night he would hold the legs of the pyjamas ready at the right angle for Ken to step into them.

Abdul was a Muslim and spoke quite good English before they arrived. The obvious thing was for Ken to teach him more, and for Abdul to help Ken with Hindustani, or Urdu. Abdul could also type, and learned everything very rapidly, almost anticipating their needs, such as fetching Jo's compact from the top of her dressing-table.

At the earliest possible moment, Jo went over the layout of the bungalow in detail with Ken. It had a large living-room, a dining-room, their bedroom, dressing-room, and the huge bathroom leading off it. All the rooms had access from outside for the boys to bring in water, which was not laid on by pipe.

Dehra Dun was half hill-station, almost in the category of Bangalore, housing an Indian military academy, the depot of the 2nd/9th Gurkha Rifles, the well-known Dun School, a hospital, and detachments of the Beds and Herts Regiment and the Royal Irish Fusiliers. It had an agreeable climate, and they spent part of Christmas Day on the flat roof of the bungalow. It was hot in the sun and cool in the shade, yet never muggy. Often in the evenings an open fire was wanted, and off-duty Ken sometimes wore a tweed suit. From Dehra Dun, Jo could see and describe to Ken the evening lights of the hill-stations twinkling on the lower slopes of the Himalayas. Later on, they went up there on pleasant picnics.

St Dunstan's had taken over some buildings at Dehra Dun for the Indian war blinded. At an informal tea-party there, Ken and Jo were introduced to curry puffs as well as to the local leading lights.

Ken concentrated as usual on the general geography of the compound and the relationship of their home to it, so that he would be able to get about alone. He had one of the four offices in the bungalow block from which the institution was run. He discovered early on the complications in the organization caused by having to keep the various religious sects separate, and even provide different cookhouses for them. One or two of the castes would not eat food if the shadow of someone from a lower caste had fallen across it. So, catering proved quite involved in proportion to the small number of blinded there – less than a hundred.

One of the basic problems for St Dunstan's had been overcome once the men agreed actually to join, for it often turned out to be a hard job persuading an Indian and his family that it was not the divine will that he should remain helpless. This fatalistic attitude to the disability was still common throughout India, and, of course, many cases had occurred of parents intentionally blinding one of their children, so that they could use the unfortunate victim as a means of making money by begging. This mentality marked a world of difference from the civilized outlook at Church Stretton, but St Dunstan's could only try to bring enlightenment to as many as could be converted.

With his experience of learning the symbols evolved during the transcription into braille of the textbook in London, Ken could contribute quite a lot to one of the problems facing St Dunstan's or whoever took over blind welfare in India from the society: to devise a braille code for Oriental languages. No braille printing at all was undertaken in India, but the need had become urgent for such a code based on the six-dot braille system, yet able to interpret all the extra sounds in such languages as those spoken in Southern India. These Eastern languages are not based on the Roman alphabet of twenty-six letters, and the aim was to perfect and present a code of braille symbols to denote all the various sounds of these languages.

Sir Clutha Mackenzie, a European captain who spoke Oriental languages fluently, and Ken evolved a code to satisfy as many tongues as possible, but Ken could not stay in India long enough to have the satisfaction of knowing it had been adopted and used. They got all the unusual guttural tones in it, and felt fairly pleased with the result. The final fruition would only come, however, with the setting up in India of a braille printing house providing literature in their own language. But while Ken was at Dehra Dun, only one man attempted to read braille, presumably because even if others did so they would not understand the English words when they had transcribed them. On this work, Ken got to know Sir Clutha Mackenzie better; he was a New Zealander who had been blinded at Gallipoli, in the First World War, so he himself had been a St Dunstaner, too.

The practical training for the Indian Army blinded was naturally more elementary than in England, and consisted largely of teaching them a craft. Making rope and baskets were obviously suitable as traditional crafts, and they also plaited mats and made webbing. All the craft instructors were sighted Indians, and Ken's job was to help Sir Clutha on the welfare side by going round to check how they were getting on and to encourage them.

Since the average Indian, even at St Dunstan's, still thought of blindness as an affliction to be accepted and borne rather than a challenge to be overcome, Ken's job proved more demanding than it sounded. They still seemed too close to the 'begging-bowl' state of mind in some cases, and he never quite knew what to expect next. One of them regularly turned out without his trousers on! No one ever discovered why this was.

Ken started as he meant to go on, by finding his own way from the bungalow, through a gateway in the wall, to a guiding rail, and so along a gravel drive to the office block. This rail had been installed between the men's huts and the centre of the compound, so that they could walk or run around it on the drive for exercise without any help or chance of hurting themselves.

Ken got to know the Gurkhas from Nepal, the Hindus, the Sikhs and Muslims, always remembering the distinction between the Gurkhas and the rest. They were known as G.O.R.s, Gurkha Other Ranks, and the rest as I.O.R.s, Indian Other Ranks.

He met one of the most poignant cases in the compound quite soon after his arrival, an affliction that made Ken realize once more that things might be worse for him than they were. This young man was about twenty-two, and as well as being blinded had been otherwise injured while serving in the Army. He had lost both his hands. So, each morning he was led into Ken's office by a guide, since he could not open doors for himself or protect himself properly without hands. They had already devised a modified typewriter for him. Over the normal keyboard fitted a special cover, and on his arms, he had angled stumps attached to leather cups. With these stumps, he could tap along a particular bank of keys, and by means of the special cover fitting count the nicks from the left and know which letter to depress. He had to have the paper put into the machine for him, naturally, and also removed afterwards.

Ken wondered if he really did get any satisfaction from such a small achievement. Yet perhaps it was something after all. Certainly, it made Ken himself feel far less handicapped when he realized that he could type a letter to his parents back in England, address an envelope, seal it, stick on a stamp, and post it, all alone. So, there were degrees of disability even in blindness – and, perhaps, degrees of compensation as well. He felt duly thankful for the mercies he had.

The Indian remained fairly cheerful considering his condition, and Ken spent some time with him regularly, helping with his English and at the same time improving his own Urdu.

Ken made a particular point of taking the man for walks, together with a bright little guide who could see. The guide led the two of them, one on each arm, and they set off for tours all round the neighbourhood of Dehra Dun. As soon as the guide saw something interesting, he would call out and they would all discuss it in both languages. Or if Ken caught the sound of a stream, he told them all the words he could think of which were connected with it: stream, water, bridge, bank. Strangely enough, this handless Indian was the only one Ken came in contact with at the compound who could make himself understood at all in English.

So, Ken settled down into the easy routine of Dehra Dun, getting acclimatized not only to the weather but to the strange sounds that were his chief source of impressions. They had several portable record players that they liked to play in the compound, and the weird strains of Indian flute and drum music often wafted into Ken's little office. One day, too, while he was just finishing playing a record to one or two men in the office, he shut the lid down and caught some one's finger in it unwittingly!

Every few days, too, there would be a proper Gurkha band concert on the lawn, and Ken was never sure which seemed stranger – the Oriental music or this slightly Scottish pipe-and-drum band. He liked to ask Jo about the scene on days like these, and visualized the smart soldierly Gurkhas and the colourful saris of the women watching and listening.

As a change from music and crafts, remembering that variety was prominent in the Church Stretton policy, Ken gave the men some friendly talks about England and English ways. These were negotiated mainly through an interpreter, who also acted as liaison between Ken and anyone asking him questions. Gradually, almost unconsciously, Ken was changing from someone needing help into a man to whom others turned for help themselves.

Another part of his time was taken up by dictating appeals letters to various organizations in India for St Dunstan's. Societies, Army units, and private individuals all sent a steady flow of cheques and money in response to these letters and advertisements in *The Times of India*, and other publications. Ken had a secretary for outside typing, but he did type in the office for internal circulation or his own benefit. He also used a braille writer when he wanted to make a written record of something he might need to refer to later.

After the effort of the office, he was always glad to get home to Jo, the palatial bungalow, and the indispensable Abdul. One evening Jo suddenly asked him, "Can I have a dog again, Ken?"

She had reared several in the past, the last being the Alsatian puppy Sheba, who had disgraced herself on the floor of the Newhaven landlady's house! Jo had sent Sheba off to be trained as a guide dog after Ken's accident, but she got distemper and hardpad, and had to be destroyed. Jo missed her very much and wanted another like her. Ken agreed at once, and it did not take Jo long to find a black bitch puppy. Knowing how Alsatians are inclined to be one-person animals, Jo suggested to Ken soon afterwards, "Why don't you have one too?"

So, Ken acquired an Alsatian brindle bitch pup, with a less impressive pedigree than the black Alsatian. When they got her home, they found that the two bitches would not agree at all, and had to be separated. So, Jo bought a baby-pen which she used for dividing the bathroom into separate halves, where the pups had their meals. They were duly christened Lorraine (Jo's) and Delilah (Ken's), and made lively additions to the Revis menage. One small operation was called for before Delilah attained perfection. She had a curly tail when they bought her, so Ken got the local vet to put it in a plaster-of-Paris tube to set it straight. This did not hurt the large pup, and was only like bending a sapling to the correct shape. While she had the plaster on, the tail plumped out straight on the floor every time she sat down, but the setting could soon be removed to reveal a smart straight tail! When Ken and Jo had to leave India, they sold the dogs to a maharajah for his wife, who was keen to have some Alsatians. That did not mean the end of dogs for them, however, and two or three years later Sandra entered the scene. But she is another story.

Meanwhile, the social life raced on at Dehra Dun. Ken had some clothes made to measure for himself out there in record time to help keep up with this whirl of activity. A suit and sports coat took the tailor a mere two days to make, while sandals could be individually cut and made within twenty-four hours. A pair Ken ordered then during 1946 refuse to wear out fifteen years later!

There were wonderful parties in the Service messes and private houses, at which Ken kept up his dancing, and Jo could describe to him tables filled with such splendours as a dozen sucking-pigs, plus mangoes and a mass of other Oriental fruits.

They belonged to the local European club, too, but Ken could not really become reconciled to this idea of exclusivity. They were in India, yet no Indians were allowed as members of the club. It seemed very strange. For the two of them had got to know and like a number of

Indians around the town, many wealthy and educated. In fact, they always seemed to be out somewhere, or else having people to the bungalow for tea or drinks on the verandah and lawn. The Indians spoke perfect English and had perfect manners, and Ken could not help feeling strongly sympathetic to their growing claims for independence.

This was approaching nearer and nearer now. Stafford Cripps had laid the foundation for it. Lord Louis Mountbatten was the last Viceroy. Already the situation had become tense, and there were isolated instances of violence between whites and Indians. Ken just could not comprehend the attitude of some Europeans, who believed that they could treat a man as badly as they liked for the sole and simple reason that he had a dark skin. Independence was inevitable. Outwardly, however, relations between the British and Indian Governments were good, and Ken actually met an Indian Housing Minister and took him on a conducted tour of St Dunstan's.

Amid all this talk of independence, however, a formal victory celebration was held in the town, and St Dunstan's took their own part in the parade. A general was taking the salute at a base, and the St Dunstan's contingent consisted of all the men, who stood up and filled two open lorries. There must have been about thirty in each. Mackenzie held on to the front rail of the leading lorry, while Ken occupied the same position in the second one. Sir Clutha was wearing his uniform and the insignia of lieutenant-colonel.

The weather was scorching as the procession wound across the parade square of Dehra Dun, and then the main complication arose as they trundled up to the saluting base at a steady speed. Ken could not see when they would be abreast the general, yet he had to give the order for recognition, so he arranged with the driver of the lorry to tip him off just before they reached the base to allow him time to call the command. The driver watched the first lorry get up to the spot, and then, just as his own lorry was approaching, he told Ken. The thirty men were all standing smartly at the back of the open lorry, gripping the side rails, as Ken called out to them:

"Eyes right."

There was not one eye among them which could see, but they all turned their heads towards the base.

After the procession there came a gymkhana, with tent-pegging contests and rescuing-the-maiden and all the other strange events of an Indian gymkhana.

The spring of 1946 scorched on. Sometimes at night in the bungalow they heard a pack of jackals wailing and whining right up to the front door, and when the night guard was not available, Ken used to go out with his stick and bang it until they went away again. One night they heard a panther come into the compound next door, and heard next day that it had made off with one of the neighbour's dogs. The bungalow was on the edge of a jungle Ken would never see.

About this time, Ken was having slight trouble with both his nose and eyes. The nose started to show some inflammation, and the doctor out there did what he could to cure it. His eyes were worse, with a definite virus in his eyelids. His artificial eyes had never completely settled down, and he felt a regular soreness in the sockets. The doctor took a swab and prescribed drops to pacify them.

Jo by now was helping to run the little mess, used by the braille teacher, the matron, her assistant, and Ken. But the political situation seemed to be taking definite shape at last, and it became clear that with independence the Indians wanted to run their own institutions as part of the country's social services. They were grateful for what St Dunstan's had done, but the time for their help was nearing an end. The ships back to Britain were already full of people leaving India, and so Ken and Jo, too, reluctantly had to think of leaving. The Indian idyll had been shorter than they hoped, but by now they were philosophic about most things.

The station staff officer at the Army H.Q., Dehra Dun, who arranged transfers and movements, phoned Bombay one day to ask the prospects of places for them on any ships, and by a lucky stroke got berths within a month. It seemed sad when they had just got used to life out there. Abdul insisted on accompanying them all the way to Bombay to help with the baggage. The handsome, round-faced Indian wanted to come to England with them, but it did not really seem possible.

So, the Bombay Mail steamed out of Dehra Dun. At wayside stations Abdul fetched food and drink for them, but once or twice they got out for a stretch as well. About half-way, Ken and Jo were strolling down the track a little way from the last carriage when, without warning, it calmly drew out.

"My God, the train's moving," Jo said. "Hold my arm, we'll have to run for it!"

They set off side by side, with Ken clutching her. The train was moving at about running speed as they heaved abreast of it. Jo spotted the running-board and an open door, so made a grab for the upright hand-holds. But it was Ken who got aboard first and hauled her up! Both breathless, they burst out laughing. The Bombay Mail only ran once a day, so they would have had a long wait for the next one.

The troopship slid up the Clyde. Jo stood at the rail watching pale pastel hills drifting into the distance. They survived a smallpox scare, which delayed things for a day while everyone was inoculated, and then they headed home for Sleaford and the family reunions. A welcoming wire from Sir Ian Fraser suggested that Ken drop in and visit him in London at a convenient time after he had settled down again. So, Ken took advantage of the offer to call on Sir Ian and discuss India and also the future.

"Well, what are you going to do now?" Sir Ian asked him.

Ken said that he would be glad of any ideas.

"Perhaps Lord Nuffield can use you. I'll write and ask him."

It sounded interesting to Ken.

Sir Ian kept his word and wrote to Nuffield, telling him that Ken was back from St Dunstan's in India and asking if he would consider employing him. Back came Nuffield's reply. Fraser phoned Ken to tell him that Nuffield suggested an interview with Sir Miles Thomas at Oxford a few days later. Accordingly, a St Dunstan's consultant travelled with Ken up to Oxford to see Sir Miles. The interview was comparatively short, and after the introductory remarks, Sir Miles asked Ken what he could do.

"I can read braille and type," Ken said, after mentioning his other qualifications.

Sir Miles thought for a moment or two.

"Well, we're willing to take you on, but I can't really give you a particular appointment at this stage. I suggest that you join personnel. Nose around and learn that side of the business, and see if you can find a niche for yourself."

Ken did not want charity. He needed a real job, and hoped it would work out all right in time. An office was a good place for a blind person. Some office jobs could be done almost entirely by telephone. Ken often thought of his life as a series of phone-calls. When a sighted person speaks to someone on the telephone whom they have not met, they get an impression of the other's appearance and character. This happens to Ken with everyone he meets. And, of course, he also finds that people who have talked quite naturally to him over the telephone change altogether when they are introduced to him face to face. There is nothing to denote to anyone that they are speaking to a blind person on the phone, so they behave naturally. When confronted with blindness, however, they become embarrassed and ill at ease. All this Ken was gradually learning.

Before he had a chance to start work, Ken renewed his acquaintance with hospitals. He was having more than his share of suffering, but he always remembered he might so easily have been killed instead of blinded. While still at Sleaford, his nose started to feel very tender

117

once more, and he was glad they were in England and not still abroad. He fingered it gently around the area where the tantalum bridge had been inserted, and it seemed as if it were being pushed out. The tantalum should have knit to the bone in the rest of the nose, but now, although there was no wound, it was definitely being forced down through his nostril.

For a few days Ken left it, but eventually his nose started to swell up violently. Quite suddenly it grew terribly inflamed and painful, and Ken could feel the metal distinctly. He got through to Professor Kilner's plastic-surgery unit at Stoke Mandeville at once and told them what was happening.

"You'd better get down here as quickly as you can. Today, if possible."

Ken and Jo threw some things into the faithful little Ford Eight and drove over to Stoke Mandeville. He went straight into an available bed after thorough washing, and had a preliminary injection. Ward 15 and Sister O'Shea were both familiar to Ken after all his previous operations, and he felt quite happy about things. Within an hour or so of arrival, he was once more being wheeled to the operating theatre which he had visualized so often. They split his nose right across the centre between the nostrils, folded it up, and removed the offending tantalum. So now for a while Ken was back where he had been, with a nose collapsed into his face. He was released from hospital with a dressing over the nose only two or three days after the operation, with the order to return within a month for the major work of creating a new nose-bridge. The time had to elapse to let the wound settle and the blood vessels vitalize. Patience was one virtue at least learned by anyone involved in plastic surgery.

Sister O'Shea greeted him back to Ward 15 for the operation to transfer part of a rib to form a bridge for his nose. Then came the shaving of his entire body for the operation, careful cleaning with ether, covering with antiseptic pads and the usual injection. But this time Ken knew next to nothing about it, for he had a general anaesthetic. They removed a piece from the back of a rib, part cartilage and part bone, shaped it into a bridge, and inserted it to form the new nose.

Ken came round in the ward and felt an enormous plaster on his face, several times the size of the nose. This had to be kept on for a fortnight till the nose had set into shape. Ken tapped it gently to investigate, and felt it as hard as the plaster on the puppy's tail in India. Breathing through his nose was difficult after all his operations, and this seemed worse than usual. But still worse was the pain in his chest. Each time he inhaled and expanded his lungs, it pressed against the tender area of removed rib. Clearing his throat was absolute agony, and he literally dare not cough after one absent-minded moment when he did so and nearly fainted with the pain.

Eventually the endless fortnight passed and the plaster came off to leave a circular block over his nose down its full extent. The moment at last arrived for this to be gently eased off, exposing the new nose for the first time. Ken was allowed to feel it and expressed amazement at its smooth surface, even at that early stage. He hoped that this time the new portion would knit on to the bone in the upper nose better than the tantalum had done. Meanwhile, with the left nostril still smaller than the right, he had to keep nose drops by the bed to clear it whenever there was any blockage. Later on, both sinuses were pierced and drained, and he received electrical treatment to assist his nasal breathing.

The big chest scar remained very painful, making breathing hard there for some time afterwards. Physiotherapy gradually helped him, however, by means of daily breathing exercises and massage.

Oxford would be their new home city. But the snag was to find their new home. They made the usual round of agents and friends, but no accommodation seemed to exist at all. St Dunstan's helped out as an emergency, for an ex-officer blinded in the First World War let them stay with him for a few weeks. Ken, of course, was also an ex-officer again, having relinquished his commission on his return from India. Soon after this, they managed to get half a small house to rent, but a living-room and bedroom with the rest of the rooms shared was no solution permanently. Then, with the year nearly over, they bought a small semi-detached house in the Cowley area and prepared for that worst winter of all – 1946-47.

But Ken could not seem to get to the end of operations. A while after his nose and chest had healed, a strange thing developed. As the central ridge of the nose had been flattened over, a piece of cartilage had forced its way through and was sticking down the right nostril. This became visible rather objectionably as a pinky-red lump whenever anyone looked at him from a lower angle than the nose. It was also beginning to get very tender, and prevented him from blowing his nose properly. Since this right-hand side was the clearer of the two nostrils, Ken wanted to keep it as free as he could, and so asked if anything could be done about it.

Into hospital he went again. They blocked up his nose with a sort of stiffener, and gave him a general anaesthetic. After the operation to remove the obstruction, they packed the nose solid again to allow it to heal, removed the packing after about a week, and then dressed it.

Ken really thought that he must have finished with his nose and hospitals for a few years at least. But no.

Soon after, they broke it to him that his tonsils had to be removed. Before the operation they anaesthetized him to block the nose with yards of bandage soaked in grease. These were packed to stop blood-clots forming and solidifying. The tonsils came out. Ken recovered consciousness. A week went by. Then the packing came out. It was a ghastly feeling for him as the bandages were pulled out of his nose, releasing a rush of filthy fluid blood. That was the end of hospitals – for ten years, anyway.

Chapter 9

SANDRA BY MY SIDE

On 10 September 1946, three years to the day after Ken's accident, he started his new job under Alex Goddard in the personnel department of Morris Motors at Oxford. At the same time, he renewed the application he had made before going to India for a guide dog. Sandra was born just about then, but another year or more had to pass before she was trained as a guide dog. Ken could not know yet just how much she would mean to him.

Meanwhile, he had a lot to learn about the organization. One of the business-training courses run by the Government for ex-Servicemen happened to involve a period spent seeing Morris Motors works, so Ken joined this more or less unofficially as a good chance to get familiar with industry and business. They attended lectures by everyone from the stock control and sales managers to the chief buyer, and also had a few days at the local technical school in Oxford. The others concluded their course in two or three weeks, but Ken got an extended version, learning about all aspects of the firm, particularly relating to personnel and welfare. Before he could be of service to them, he obviously had to learn the ropes.

Ken was naturally interested in the disabled staff at Morris Motors, who have always employed well above the legal minimum number. Then he learned about the firm's other welfare activities. Anyone taken ill while at work was automatically transported home by car free. Staff were paid in full for at least thirteen weeks when ill, and there were also pension and benevolent funds and a hospital scheme. Ken learned a lot from Fred Dudley, the welfare officer at that time, and helped him with his work on finding accommodation for the staff, organizing the appointments for the barber's shop, and keeping an artificial eye on the various benevolent schemes. Yet another job for Ken was to run the group schemes for A.A. and R.A.C. membership. All employees were entitled to this at a reduced fee, and Ken had to be sure that all the subscriptions were paid at the right time to qualify for this concession.

It was the practice of the firm to give an induction talk to everyone joining them. This was a welcoming chat telling employees all about the firm's history and activities, about the various welfare and other schemes in existence for their benefit, and the general details of sports, canteens, and other essential facts. In fact, all an employee should know to get the most out of the firm and to meet every emergency. The requirements concerning medical certificates were an important point as well.

Ken listened to this induction talk a number of times, and eventually took over the task of delivering it himself – a duty that lasted for several years. He found he was faced with anything from one to forty or fifty entrants, some new to factory life altogether and bewildered by it at first. The talk went on for the best part of an hour by the time all the amenities and topics had been mentioned. So, every new employee had the unusual experience of being welcomed to Morris Motors by a blind person who had learned all the activities of the firm.

Incidentally, at this Cowley factory, not only six blind workers were employed, but 220 other disabled persons, including two legless men in the same department. Both blind and disabled handled their particular parts of vehicle assembly with skill virtually equal to sighted people, even applying the smallest bolts and washers accurately. Some of those who were blind assembled instrument fascia panels for cars quickly, leaving them ready to be collected for incorporation into the vehicles the following day. Most of these men had learned panel assembly from the National Institute for the Blind. They were escorted to the canteen a little before the rest of the workers, and allowed to leave early in the evening to avoid the rush on buses home.

So, Ken settled down into the daily routine, and began to make a place for himself in the vast concern. Yet another aspect of his work was devoted to solving, or advising on, the personal problems of staff. So here again there was the rare sight of a blind man helping ordinary people with their lives. Ken got all sorts of strange cases, from straightforward legal queries to a husband who asked him, "What shall I do, Mr Revis? My wife has been lured away by another man."

Ken could not claim to solve such basic complexities, but wherever possible he did smooth things out, often with the help of a phone call to the proper person. He came to rely more and more on the telephone as something he could really use on equal terms with ordinary people. He liked meeting all the staff, and especially getting to know the men in the factory itself. He developed an almost uncanny ear for voices, and could really boast of being able to tell practically anyone's voice which he had heard two or three times. With friends and business acquaintances, this began to run into large numbers. That first year passed with a firm's car taking Ken to and from work, but then Sandra came on to the scene.

Ken and Jo had originally applied for a guide dog while at Church Stretton, before they knew about going to India. At that time, they had gone to see Captain Nicolai Liakhoff, head of the Guide Dogs for the Blind Association, at the training centre near Leamington Spa. Liakhoff always liked to see the applicants before settling anything, so that he knew what they were like. On the form, therefore, Ken had to give all his details, such as height and weight; whether or not he walked with a stick; if he was completely blind or could distinguish light; how fast or slow was his gait. A large man obviously needs a different dog from that of a small woman. Alsatian bitches are best of all, though most large breeds can be trained as guide dogs. Boxers, Labradors, and Collies have all been successfully used, but the vital thing has always been to get the right dog for the right person. As Liakhoff put it, "We are uniting the eyes of an animal with the mind of a human being." Ken thought of it as walking with a stranger in the city of Oxford, except that the dog would not be able to talk or read street-names.

There are different types of people among those who are blind, just as among the rest of humanity. A common tendency is to overlook this, and lump every one blind as exactly the same. Some are better, others worse; some handier, others more awkward; some have a sense of humour, others do not. Liakhoff took all the things he could into consideration before deciding which dog to allocate to a particular person. For, of course, dogs also have their own characteristics, which must be matched, if possible, to the intended owner.

Finally, in December 1947, Ken got a letter from Liakhoff inviting him up to the training centre. They had trained a dog for him already over the previous three months, but the next step was to familiarize guide with owner, so that they acted as one. Not so automatic as it might sound in theory.

Jo drove Ken up to Leamington and helped him with his unpacking in the bedroom. She told him where things were, and generally explained the geography and the way from his room down to the common-room. Then she had to go. Ken found himself on his own once more, a stranger in the house, with all its odd pitfalls of unfamiliar steps and turnings he could not know. He was not really alone, though, for each session six dogs were prepared for six students, of which he was one. Ken arrived in company with a piano-playing Yorkshireman, a Clacton housewife, a man named Robinson, a Polish doctor whom Ken believed had been blinded in the war, and a South African who had definitely received his injury during the war and afterwards attended St Dunstan's. Nothing happened that day, except meals served by the kennel-maids, who told them all where the cruet and water was on the table and allowed them to use their own initiative to find them.

Next morning, with all of them grouped around the common-room fire chatting, several of the trainers came in, and one said, "Perhaps you'd like to meet your dogs."

There was general excitement as they were each given a handful of minced meat on a paper ready to feed the animals when they entered. Then the door burst open and half a dozen dogs panted into the room. No one knew which was which, nor could anyone see to sort it out. So, they had to hold their meat high in the air out of reach till the trainers quietened the dogs down a bit.

Ken knew Sandra was a white Alsatian bitch, although some of the others still had no idea of the breed they would be allotted. Then he heard a voice saying, "Here you are, Mr Revis, this is yours. Come on, Sandra."

Ken and Sandra did not know each other. It was different three weeks later. Just then, however, the only importance of Ken to her was the handful of meat he still held up high. He gripped her collar while she ate the meat, and they let him pat and play with her. Ken realized then that when someone cannot see a dog it is not always easy to recognize it until they know each other. For the first few hours, he found it hard to tell which was Sandra, once he had lost her collar and let her roam around the room. To begin with, he recognized her by feeling all the dogs till he came to one with a big "tummy button!" And that was Sandra.

Ken was actually responsible for feeding Sandra from the start, either giving the food to her himself or accompanying a kennel-maid. He took the meat and baked bread to her kennel, and after about only the first day she started to get excited and recognize him.

He felt so proud of her right from that first meeting, for Sandra was the only pure white guide dog in the country at the time. Already Ken had learned about her breed. Contrary to some people's belief, Alsatians are not fierce, nor do they have any wolf strain in them; it is only excessive confinement and lack of exercise which may make them seem nervous. So, this breed need not be feared at all, and anyone feeling like that about them is really only prejudiced.

Furthermore, the association always ensured that guide dogs were perfect before being accepted for training. Several hundred a year were received at Leamington, yet at that time only about one in five finally qualified as guides, the remainder having to be reluctantly rejected.

On the first day, training started with Ken's trainer, Betty Bridge, not the dog herself. They went out to teach Ken how to follow the harness implicitly, and so follow the dog's movements. Betty took him out with a small square leather grip to simulate a harness, and Ken took hold of it with his left hand well down by his side all the time. The dog is always on a blind person's left. Then Betty walked, swivelled, trotted, and generally moved around to get Ken used to this blind faith in following the harness, which took quite a bit of learning. They did it for several minutes, before Sandra came into the scheduled activities.

Betty explained exactly how to put on Sandra's harness. It went over her back and across her chest, just under the collar, and strapped around her stomach. Ken had to make sure that its buckles were loose and the straps under her belly not too tight. He checked by running his fingers along till he could feel between the straps and her stomach.

The harness was U-shaped and so stiff that he could pull or push it without its yielding. When Sandra stopped, he had to feel it at once. So, with the breast-band and everything firmly secured, Ken was ready to start. He practised calling her to his left.

"Come, Sandra," he repeated as he banged his left thigh with his open hand. Then he put his hand down, and she would come round to him from wherever she was, in whichever position she had been at the moment.

"Hupup," he encouraged her. This was the general term of approval.

Another early command to be taught was "Rest." With Sandra at his side, Ken held up the forefinger of his right hand and said slowly, "Rest."

Then he walked around in front of the dog, to see that she would still sit at that certain spot. The next thing was to walk away from her. Although the natural tendency would be for Sandra to get up and follow him, she had been trained to stay exactly where she was put after the order "Rest." At a reasonable distance, Ken called out "Come," and she bounded over to him in two or three giant-like leaps.

Later on, he developed this further in a football field by depositing her between a pair of goal-posts and holding his finger up as he told her to stay there. Then he would walk right away out of sight and wait three or four minutes before speaking.

"Come, Sandra."

She streaked across the pitch and almost skidded turning the corner of the wall which hid him.

The other important command which reassured Ken during those initial days at Leamington was the simple one: "Stop." He did not have to use it often, but he knew nevertheless that it was always there if he really felt for any reason he could not go on any farther. He did not have to tug Sandra to a standstill; just the one word sharply spoken was sufficient to stop her dead in her course.

So, with such basic rules as Forward, Left, Right, Sit, Rest, Come, and Stop, Ken began to feel that it might be possible after all to get about with the help of a dog. Yet the idea took quite a time to feel natural, which was not so surprising.

The first real activity to be taught was walking. Sandra, Ken, and Betty all went out along a Leamington street for this trial run. When they reached a suitable stretch of pavement Betty told Ken to get ready for this moment of launching. He made the dog stand on his left, checked that all her harness felt comfortably fitting, and then experimented at holding both the harness and the leash at the same time. Until this moment, Sandra had been on the leash, which she understood as being *off* duty. Then, as soon as Ken raised up the harness, she knew she was on duty.

Ken fiddled about a minute getting the leash tucked under his finger, while he gripped the harness as well. Then as he swept his right arm ahead of him he said, "Forward," and they were off. They could hardly be expected to be in perfect harmony yet, as Sandra had never seen Ken till the previous day. Ken's mind reeled as the dog trotted off at a fast pace, which he found hard to equal. He was experiencing his very first lesson at learning to trust an animal not to lead him into anything. I've been bumped into brick walls and other obstacles by human beings allegedly leading me, so what about a dog? Can I trust her?

He had no option, actually, as she careered forward.

"You're doing all right," Betty comforted him.

Then Sandra's attention wavered and wandered for a second, and he had to jerk the harness to get her going steadily again.

"Now you're going to come up to the kerb," Betty warned. "Be careful."

Ken gripped the harness a bit tighter and waited for the shock. Sandra stopped rather clumsily, causing him to halt too suddenly as well. Then they did it again, and again. Her fore paws reached the edge of the kerb, leaving Ken the length of the harness to stop – about one pace. Several times they tried this, getting a bit better all the while, for Sandra had to be taught being with Ken, just as he had to learn from scratch.

So, they practised walking and stopping on the edge of the kerb at a turning. The next step was actually into the road.

126

"Forward," Ken called to her, and Sandra walked quickly across the road, pausing just before the step-up on the other side to show him where it was. This they did many times, too, during the early days of the course, for Ken to gain confidence in the dog and get used to her reactions. He also had to know instinctively the pressures involved. A dog between one-third and one-half his own weight had to slow him down or stop him. That took practice to perfect, so that he did not blunder too far forward or hurt her at all.

Kerb drill came on the curriculum every morning and afternoon, and in time he gradually learned to stop efficiently as near the kerb as he could. Then there were the details of appreciating how to avoid turning towards the dog too much and risk kicking her. Ken had to walk straight, with his arm down at his side, so that he kept the same width of dog-plus-man, otherwise Sandra could not know where she was or how much space to allow for them both.

To help her further in this problem, the next little idea was obstacle drill. This took place in the grounds of the manor-house headquarters of the training centre, and consisted of dog and man passing between hurdles in the form of lightly built fences on stands. These were staggered cunningly to try to test the dog to the extreme, but Sandra gradually got the hang of it, and allowed wide enough clearance for both herself and Ken to get by without touching them. The obstacles were set up at every possible angle, so that Sandra really had to keep her wits lively while Ken gamely followed her changing courses.

If she did make a slight mistake and he touched a hurdle, he had to jerk her so that she knew. When she really made a bad blunder Ken had strict orders to admonish her with the standard word and gesture for the purpose: "Phooooey" with his finger held up and a jerk on the harness.

So, they improved. Sandra was between fifteen and eighteen months old when Ken took his training, so had reached maturity. She was old enough to be trained well, and the theory was that although a dog does not reason, training builds on her innate abilities. So, she got to know their combined width and acted instinctively as if she had a large extension of herself on her right.

Or as Ken put it on her behalf: "That old fool on my right!"

When she was particularly bright, he praised her with "Good girl" and patted her. Their friendship was deepening already, and together they advanced to the traffic training, which really put it to the test and proved it.

This was undertaken with Ken, Sandra, and two trainers. Betty stayed on the pavement near Ken and Sandra, while the other trainer drove a car. Betty told Ken to go forward along a particular pavement until they reached the kerb on a side turning, where the other trainer was waiting in a parked car. At a given signal from Betty, the driver moved off towards the point where Ken was standing. Then Betty told Ken to cross.

"Forward," he told Sandra.

But she disobeyed him.

She had seen the approaching car and was trained only to obey the command when the road was quite clear. This was a marvellous moment for Ken as he patted Sandra. He suddenly realized how she could become his eyes, and save him from harm. The dog did not budge until the car was safely past, then she stepped off across the road confidently. They did that many times during the three weeks. It really does work, Ken thought.

Training always has to be maintained, built on, for a dog is only flesh and blood and not an automaton. Any tendency to go forward at all when traffic was about, had to be checked at once. Then they went on to another road and repeated the test frequently.

The difficulty of fooling a dog was demonstrated in this test, however, for after a while Sandra started to recognize the car and the driver, and was inclined to look on it all as a game. So, the cars and drivers had to be changed often, and the drill gone over again and again, like barracks-square movements, until Ken had complete confidence that she would always stop if she saw any oncoming traffic.

By now he was about three-quarters of the way through the course, and had graduated to a walk on his own. They handed him an embossed map of the immediate district, which he memorized. Then he was shown a particular circular route on this map, which he also had to commit to memory. He did not take the map with him for reference, but trusted to remembering the route – and Sandra.

Sandra, of course, did not know which way they were going, and would walk straight ahead unless ordered to do otherwise. It was up to Ken to *tell* her otherwise. If he lost the way he could always listen for footsteps and ask for directions, but he hoped that would not be necessary. So, he set off with the names of the streets in his mind as well as the number of turnings, so that he could ask intelligently if he had to.

At the first kerb, the dog stopped. Ken counted that as the first turning, and then they crossed safely. He got to the third turning, where he had to alter course, and so on according to the instructions he had been told.

"Forward." And Sandra shot ahead again. Then another change of direction.

128

"Right," Ken said, taking half a pace backward and turning to the right. Sandra swung round, too, and continued her trot down the centre of the pavement. Second on the left. Second on the right. Eventually they got back on the main road and approached the main gates of the training centre. Sandra began to get excited, like all dogs returning home after an outing, and she swung Ken through the gates with a real swagger. He heard his feet crunching down the friendly gravel, and felt on top of the world. He was home safely after his first solo trip.

Sandra led him down the drive, and through one special door in the house. A wire was stretched between posts for Ken and the others to find their way to this back door and also to the kennels, for they groomed the dogs themselves from the first day they were introduced. Now the harness came off, and Sandra had finished her work for another day.

Towards the end of the training, Ken learned the little extras which Sandra could perform to help lighten his life. Guide dogs are taught to pick up things for their masters, and even find them whenever possible. The groundwork in this consisted of Ken taking her lead in his hand and bringing her to the left. Then he put a glove down on the ground, and pulled her neck down very gently, at the same time saying, "*Apporte*."

Sandra grabbed the glove.

"Come."

Sandra trotted round to the rear of Ken with the glove in her mouth, ready to release it into his hand. Ken took it, patted her, and then they repeated the test. Sandra naturally preferred wooden or fabric articles to metallic ones, but she would bring back to him anything he asked, to such small oddments as a collar-stud he might mislay or drop.

With the main lessons learned, Ken attended to details arising from the three weeks, like the bottom of his raincoat which flapped into Sandra sometimes while they were out walking, and seemed to put her off a bit.

Then the last day rolled round quickly, and they all assembled in the common-room for a cheerful evening. They had some drinks, listened to the Yorkshireman playing the piano, and generally had a sing-song. Ken's contribution was *Empty Saddles*, requested by Liakhoff, who was a great horseman and, in fact, seemed to be wonderful with all animals.

Back in Oxford, Ken had to set about learning the district if he were to make use of Sandra's services. It was unlucky that they lived in a place he never knew before being blinded, but as things were Jo walked with him from the little house in Cowley to the factory, through the gates, and right into his office. Jo did this for a week, telling him the names of the streets on the way and conveying the exact route to Ken.

Sandra, too, grew used to the walk to and from work and the following week Ken left home by himself, to be guided to Morris Motors, a mile away. The walk passed uneventfully, except at one stage along a narrow pavement. Sandra could not walk any nearer to the edge than she was, and yet Ken stumbled against some steps, raised in front of a cottage door. Then Liakhoff himself paid a call on Ken and walked the route with him. The keen eye of the trainer soon saw the awkward spots, and instilled them into Sandra's mind by hitting them with his stick. So, at a certain lamp-post which had proved rather an obstacle for Ken and Sandra, he gave it a sharp knock to indicate to the dog that she should take special care here. So, the man and the dog gradually got to know their way.

Ken and Sandra learned other walks as well, but if he wanted to go a special way, he had to take her in hand and say, "Come on, Sandra, *this* way."

Otherwise, Ken would find himself heading for his office on a Saturday or Sunday!

On the whole, Ken found people helpful, the policeman on the particular gate he used always held up the traffic for a second or two while Ken got clear of the actual entrance. In his office, Ken acquired a square of car carpeting and taught Sandra to lie on it during the day. The only snag was that she insisted on emitting a loud, protective bark every time anyone came into the room. Then at midday, they went across the road to the canteen for lunch. Ken usually walked with a friend at lunch-time, and so Sandra was on her lead and off duty. They strolled near the airfield and let her off for a run before she had to resume her vigil in the office for the afternoon.

As Ken wanted to get about the factory more and more, he had a plan of the whole 200-or-so acres made with cardboard blocks to indicate the actual factory sites. In this way, he could feel the direction to the various workshops. Then it was home at night, a quarter of an hour's walk with all left turns. Sometimes he got a lift, and Sandra piled into the back of the car as well, quite pleased to have a rest from her responsibilities.

After a while Ken grew more adventurous and found a quicker way home. This took him through a vast area where hundreds of new cars were parked awaiting dispatch. Then through a gate, which he locked behind him, and past the perimeter of the air-field and to the road where they lived.

One winter night the fog came down dense as Ken bumped into the labour manager, who said, "I can't see a thing, Ken."

"That's all right. Put your hands on my shoulders, and we'll let Sandra find the way out!"

So, Sandra threaded her way among the dozens of rows of cars shrouded in the white fog, while Ken held on to the harness, and the labour manager brought up the rear.

"Case of the blind leading the blind," Ken said over his shoulder. And sure enough, Sandra brought them out safely into the street.

Gradually, too, Ken trained Sandra to lead him to one or two other useful destinations, and the day came after some practice when he was able to close the gate of their house at 24 Bartholomew Road, Cowley, turn to Sandra, and say simply, "Post."

Then the beautiful white bitch with the pinkish nose and tongue hanging out would perk up her ears and lead Ken safely to the post-office. Here he could dispatch letters that he had typed privately himself, and then Sandra would set off for home again, with Ken at her side looking smart in his double-breasted blazer. By now the pair of them were becoming familiar figures in Cowley.

Ken normally travelled either by the car; walked with Sandra; went out with Jo and Sandra, or else just with Jo. At that stage no dogs were allowed on the Oxford buses, but it became clear that it would be useful for Ken to be able to go by bus occasionally when he wanted to get into the shops or somewhere alone. He really decided to try and do something about it when he started appeals work for the Guide Dogs for the Blind Association, as this would involve him in getting about the district and he did not want to have to rely on Jo every time.

He set out one day to walk the mile to the bus-station to see the manager there about allowing guide dogs on his vehicles. The hollow noise told Ken he had reached the depot, and he soon found the manager's office. It took only a short chat for the manager to agree to change the rule to allow guide dogs and owners on buses, and he assured Ken he would notify all staff accordingly. The first time Ken wanted to avail himself of a bus came when he had to get from Cowley across to the Banbury Road to talk to a meeting about guide dogs a few weeks later.

Ken never got as far as travelling on a bus at all that evening, however. As soon as one drew up at the stop and he tried to board it, the conductor called out, "No dogs allowed."

"But she's a guide dog. I'm a blind person."

"You'll have to get off. I can't let a dog on this bus."

"But I'm entitled to bring her. I've got written permission from your manager." Ken was getting annoyed now, but it was still no use.

"Well, you'll have to speak to my driver about it."

The conductor did not help him at all, but Ken managed to grope his way round the smooth side of the bus behind Sandra. The engine was roaring away all the time, and he could feel its vibration throbbing through the chassis.

"But I'm a blind person and I have permission to bring my guide dog on the bus," Ken began.

The driver stuck his head out of the window, "Can't help that, mate. No dogs allowed. Nothing I can do. Now mind out, we're late."

With that, the bus jerked forward, nearly knocking both Ken and Sandra sprawling in the gutter. He was livid by this time, and went home to tell Jo. The two of them found the manager's private address, and went straight round to call on him to explain the treatment Ken had just received.

The man was very apologetic. A few days later Ken got two letters through the post, also apologetic, one from the conductor, one from the driver.

St Dunstan's had often asked Ken to do little things for them at one time or another, perhaps giving a talk to a group of people or else receiving a cheque collected on behalf of St Dunstan's. A man at Chippenham who ran billiards tournaments for the same purpose also asked him to come and collect the money raised by one of them.

It was these tournaments that gave Ken and Jo the idea of organizing something similar in Oxford for Guide Dogs, who were badly in need of help. The first event in the campaign was, in fact, a billiards demonstration given by the famous player, Horace Lindrum, at a Cowley club.

Lindrum duly shook Sandra by the paw, and the evening's play was described to Ken by a friend. From this first modest venture the Guide Dogs fund benefited by £65 – enough encouragement for Ken and Jo to pursue the campaign regularly.

Arising out of the first show came a billiards exhibition mounted in the Oxford town-hall, with Horace Lindrum performing free for Guide Dogs. The public also saw celebrities from many other sports as well, including Henry Longhurst, Don Cockell, and McDonald Bailey. Ken had the job of introducing these guests, which he must have done quite agreeably, because Roger Eckersley, then the general manager of Guide Dogs, came over to him afterwards and asked him if he would undertake appeals work generally in the area. Eckersley was an ex–B.B.C. man whom Ken would meet again subsequently as a result of this evening. So, Ken and Jo became Oxford County organizers for the Guide Dogs for the Blind Association, and received headed notepaper appropriate to the work.

From this time on not only Ken and Jo but Sandra, too, began to become more and more known locally. They made frequent sorties, with either Jo or a Morris Motors driver at the wheel of the car, and collected considerable sums for Guide Dogs wherever they went. At a social club in Oxford, Ken was photographed very carefully placing the final penny on a tower of pennies built on the rim of a pint beer-mug! When the ring was broken up and the pennies counted, the number came to five guineas to the penny. And on these car trips, Sandra often occupied both back seats with elegance and enjoyment.

In the spring of 1952, Ken and Jo organized a ball at the Randolph Hotel, Oxford, in aid of Guide Dogs, which turned out to be a brilliant night. Ken actually gave a demonstration during the evening with Sandra. She sat, and lay down, and then jumped up and retrieved various things at his word, generally stealing the show.

And the floor-show sustained the theme of dogs, with the team of Formackin Canine Stars. These included corgis and wire-haired fox-terriers, which jumped through hoops and over hurdles to collect eggs, milk, and dishes. The audience applauded, too, as the dogs selected certain colours as commanded, and then finally a pair of corgis drew a covered wagon across the dance floor. The funds from the evening were increased still further by a cheque for £50 from Lord Nuffield, handed to Ken in the midst of the ball.

The United States Air Force from Brize Norton contributed some turns to a variety show held at Cowley soon after the ball, and it was during the interval that Ken stepped on the stage to tell the audience a little about Guide Dogs and how Sandra had returned mobility and a measure of self-respect to his life. He revealed as well that output of trained guide dogs had now doubled since the time of Sandra's training, amounting to about seventy a year. The cost to train a dog then was £225, and the waiting-list for these dogs ran to about five years. Sandra underlined all his points as she guided him off the stage.

Ken had another speaking engagement at an Oxford Rotary Club luncheon, where Sandra was, in fact, given a separate seat beside him, and sat up properly to the table for a meal with him!

And so, the work went on in Ken's spare time. Fetes, gymkhanas, garden parties, Women's Institute meetings, Red Cross affairs, and every kind of county gathering. Ken gave regular-obedience demonstrations, and Sandra always rose to the occasion as if trained to be not only a guide dog but an actress as well. She had a tremendously positive personality and zest for all her work, whether with Ken alone or before an audience.

133

It may be that her enthusiasm led her into doing more than she could really manage. Whether or not that was so, Sandra began to show signs of slowing up in the early 1950s. Ken's coaxing "Hupup, Sandra" did not do any good, and she seemed to be getting a bit careless, even lazy. They were at once worried, because by now she had proved overwhelmingly how full of life she was when feeling fit. And in addition to this, of course, any slackening in her efficiency made life dangerous for Ken.

"Something's wrong with her, I'm sure," Ken told Jo one day. "Let's get the vet to have a look at her."

Miss Ballard examined Sandra thoroughly before announcing quietly, "It's her heart. She must be rested, and I'll give her something for it."

This was an awful blow. Ken had not fully realized the integral part of his life she had become. His working day began and ended with her. She was his eyes. Still, they had no choice but to rest her, and with a heavy heart Ken went up to Leamington again.

Panda was as black as Sandra was white, and their personalities seemed equally different, too. Ken trained with her thoroughly, yet somehow, they never grew united in anything like the same way as with Sandra. She knew her training, but there was always something between them, keeping them apart. Perhaps it was the presence of Sandra. Anyway, Ken never felt fully comfortable. He summed up the difference between the two Alsatians in a simple way. Sandra would always jump to the top of the coal-bunker at the back of their house in Cowley. Panda would never get up there. She just did not have the same spirit.

But she did her best, despite the difficult situation, and took Ken to work regularly. Sandra eyed them silently. The biscuit tinge to her ears and down her back were outlined against the white of the rest of her body. She was still a beautiful dog. Even while ill, Sandra retained her personality, and Ken took her out on a little private walk in the evening to show that she had not been replaced. All this time the vet continued to treat her, and they all treated her simply as a pet, being fussed over for nearly eight months.

Ken could never really get on well with Panda, and once or twice she was inclined to swing him straight out towards the road, so that at that stage neither of the dogs could be called perfectly fit for service.

After Sandra had been visiting at the home of Jo's parents for a week or so, she returned to the fold frisky again.

"Do you think I can try Sandra again now?" Ken asked Miss Ballard one day soon afterwards.

"I don't see why not. She's recovered by now, but perhaps you ought to ask Captain Liakhoff."

Liakhoff agreed if the vet really thought Sandra was fit for it, so at last Ken could try her once more. She seemed quite cured and as ready and willing as in the old days, wagging her tail when petted by Ken or Jo, who loved her just as much as he did.

Sandra had not had the harness on for eight months, or done any of her training at all. The equivalent of four years to a man. Ken put it on her, and Jo said that she would walk to work with him once or twice to see how things went after this long gap.

Ken walked out of the gate with Sandra by his side in her old position. He had to test her at once. The kerb lay some six paces away from the gate, three to cross the path, three for the grass verge. Sandra should stop automatically before the kerb. He held his breath as they started and he took four paces. He felt the grass under his feet – and then the jolt as Sandra stopped. She still knew her work perfectly after eight months' idleness. Ken was touched.

"You needn't come," he called to Jo.

Together he and the dog walked to work, and she remembered the way in through the gate, and the door to the office block in the personnel department, where a fuss awaited her.

Ken returned Panda to Leamington. Those months had been an extra strain for him. Every blind person suffers strain just in daily routine, and any extra burden becomes disproportionately heavy. Now he had Sandra with him, and he backed up her training to help remind her of all the details in it. He never forgot that she was trying to tell him something with all her actions, and he encouraged her a lot with "Good girl," and some hefty pats. Her heart trouble seemed to be cured.

Jo realized the importance of keeping their lives as full as possible, and that was why she welcomed the appeals work, even though it did tax Ken's strength slightly. They had to resist the deadening effect of routine which any job would impart, and so took as many opportunities as they could for an odd day out. A memorable one for them both was the Coronation.

Some friends living at Stanhope Gate, near Park Lane, invited them up for the day, and Jo drove through the early hours to reach North-west London by about 4 a.m. After parking the car in a side street near Queensway, they strolled across Hyde Park in the dawn. Jo excitedly told Ken about all the sights. The mounted police with sidelights on their stirrups, and other unusual things at that hour of the morning. He caught the atmosphere easily himself, however, as Scots songs wafted over the air to the drone of bagpipes.

A little farther, he heard an accordion accompanying some drunken singing, then the general crowd noises as they reached the Park Lane area. Ken heard the television commentary, the radio description, and also popped down into the street with Jo once or twice, as well as getting firsthand reports from her most of the time. So altogether he picked up a picture pretty well as complete as most people either along the route or watching or listening at home. He could not help one or two pangs at missing a day like this, but by now he had more or less grown completely used to his dark world.

He had had nearly ten years of it, and learned that although he lost a lot, there still remained enough to make life more than worth living. The radio and television came to his help often on occasions like these. Ken loved sports commentaries, particularly of the sports he liked before his blindness. Rex Alston's rugger eye-witness accounts brought the game alive to him. Similarly with Raymond Baxter on motor-racing. While Ken listened to Baxter one day, and heard the sound-effects microphone as the cars raced round Silverstone, he recalled clearly a day he spent at Brooklands back in 1936. He drove there in his home-made car, parked it somewhere along the way from Weybridge, and then took his place in that pre-war racing course to watch the famous "500" – the 500-miles handicap race. He could smell again the exhaust and later the scent of the pine-trees. That was a day to remember, to see in his mind for as long as he lived.

Ken went to Henley, too, before the war, and eventually got into the habit of hearing the commentaries on the various events each year. For the Oxford-Cambridge boat-race itself, and similar sports broadcasts, Ken had the radio commentary on, while Jo and anyone else there watched it on television. She filled in the verbal picture if it is ever necessary, and both of them got as much as possible from it. The TV commentary alone, of course, was not enough, and so they switched the sound off. With plays and other programmes on television, however, Ken began to find that he could get a lot out of them, with the additional word or two when needed from Jo. He could not have had two livelier, devoted helpers than Jo and Sandra!

The work for Guide Dogs went on. One day in 1953, Ken was talking to some other owners about the association, and it cropped up that the twentieth anniversary would soon be due. The idea of guide dogs originally began in Germany, where animals were trained to help men blinded in the First World War. Liakhoff was training dogs in Switzerland between the wars when he was invited to come to Britain in 1933 and start a centre here. Thus started the Guide Dogs for the Blind Association in this country.

"It would be nice to do something to mark this birthday, wouldn't it?" Ken said.

From their various suggestions, the idea emerged of a luncheon in Oxford with Captain and Mrs Liakhoff as guests of honour. Then the question of presents arose, and all owners of guide dogs were circularized for contributions. Ken and Jo really organized the whole function, and about sixty of the 318 guide dog owners turned up at the Forum Restaurant, Oxford, three with their dogs as well.

Sandra was back in her best form and in the limelight as usual. Ken shone, too, while introducing the Earl of Northesk as "one of the foremost doggy men in the country." This was an apt phrase, since he was prominently associated with Cruft's, the Kennel Club, and the Tailwaggers' Club.

Lord Northesk made the presentations of an inscribed gold cigarette-case to Captain Liakhoff, and a gold wrist-watch to his wife. They were visibly moved by these gifts, especially since none of the donors contributing could witness the presentation.

With Sandra were the three other guide dogs. Mrs Dora Thompson told how her black Labrador, Daphne, took her to the theatre, the cinema, and all over London, adding "there's only one place my dog has not been allowed to enter – the House of Commons." Mr J.W. Jones, national organizer for the Old Age Pensioners' Association, brought his Alsatian, Tosca, and Mr G. Goodwin also came with an Alsatian, Serena.

The owners could not see the occasion, of course. And there was one toast to which there could be no response. It was a toast to the dogs.

Ken's activities started to spread beyond Oxfordshire to many other places, including his own home-town, where the Bedford and District Sandra Revis Guide Dog Fund was opened. The initial target of £250, to provide one trained guide dog, was easily passed, and soon reached £723, enough for three dogs. The appeal had been launched with a picture of Ken and Sandra, who was 'saying':

> My blind master is an Old Bedfordian, and I hear that my name is being used in raising funds for the Guide Dogs for the Blind Association, which is the only one of its kind in Britain. It cost about £250 to train me and my master. Yes, my master has to be trained with me. This seems a lot of money, but he says I am worth my weight in gold. We are a very happy pair. Unfortunately, there is a long waiting-list of blind people who are not so happy, but could be if sufficient funds were raised to train more guide dogs like me. That's all! Now I am off to play a ball game in the garden. We love to play when we are off duty.

Sandra made a personal appearance at Cruft's Dog Show, not as a competitor, but for the same cause – collecting towards Guide Dogs.

By a coincidence, Guide Dogs benefited as a result of a television series planned for 1955. The B.B.C. were thinking up the idea for *Top Town*, the talent contest between boroughs in the British Isles, and wrote to Oxford Corporation asking for their help. As not much co-operation seemed to be forthcoming, the B.B.C. put out personal local feelers to try to find someone who would help them get a team together to represent Oxford in a proposed match against Cambridge.

"Can I bring Billy Scott-Comber to see you, Ken?" a friend of his asked one day on the phone.

Ken and Jo had moved from Cowley into the country at Iffley by now, and Ken soon found himself talking to Scott-Comber, assistant to B.B.C. producer Barney Colehan.

"We want someone to organize a *Top Town* team here, Mr Revis. We've heard all about your various work in the area, and wondered if you'd take it on."

Ken had left Morris Motors shortly before this, and now found himself very busy in a new life, but before he could refuse or agree, Jo piped up, "Shall we try it between us, Ken?"

"O.K. – if you say so. But you'll have to do most of the work." Jo had already taken over most of his outstanding appeals work, but the prospect of this B.B.C. task seemed too exciting to miss. She still felt a bit frustrated sometimes through not being able to do much actively in the world of entertainment, and this might open all sorts of doors. In any case, what was there to lose?

"Right, that's settled then," Scott-Comber said.

From that beginning, they created a committee to find a *Top Town* team worthy of renewing the age-old struggle between the two university cities. The brainwave emerged of running a series of talent concerts in the town-hall, to be performed before a panel of judges and a normal paying-public audience. Nine of these concerts came off successfully, and from each the panel picked three people to go forward into an all-finals concert at the end of the series. An added excitement for Ken and Jo was his decision to have a shot at it as well. Ken had been singing for fun in odd public places since a long-distant dance at Bedford when he was eighteen. Then when he was in London one day after the war, he decided he wanted to make a record, so got in touch with Sir Ian Fraser in his capacity as the then chairman of St Dunstan's, who introduced him to Henry Hall.

The bandleader told Ken, "Be at the studios in Bond Street at 2 p.m."

Ken hurried down the street and arrived early. He was shown into a recording studio, where he was introduced to his accompanist at the piano, who turned out to be – Henry Hall! Ken felt slightly embarrassed at such a well-known person offering to accompany him, but managed to get through two current hits: *The Girl that I Marry* and *Golden Ear-Rings*.

His voice still preserved that pleasant blend of Bobby Howes and Bing Crosby, as he won one of the three places in his elimination concert. Some weeks later, at the finale, Ken caught the real atmosphere of the theatre as he heard Billy Scott-Comber and Barney Colehan timing the acts with their stop-watches. Ken sang four songs that night: *Under the bridges of Paris, C'est magnifique,* one of Bing Crosby's old records *Thanks,* and then a very special number. Roger Eckersley had written a song specially for Ken and his dog, and called it, of course, *Sandra*. Ken put all he had into his last song, with its lines like "Sandra by my side." And she was beside him on the stage all the time.

Seven winners were announced; three more to come. Then another winner. Two more. Ken wondered if he would be lucky. He heard Barney Colehan say, "And we're going to ask Ken Revis to sing *Sandra* on *Top Town.*"

Guide Dogs profited by about £500 from these ten concerts.

Next came the rehearsals for the *Top Town* show itself. Singers, dancers, jugglers, even a cartoonist, and Ken and Sandra. First rehearsals were arranged in small groups in halls close to the artists' homes.

Their new house was named Mallows, after the first officers' mess Ken knew at Haywards Heath. He remembered it as approached by a circular drive. And the house had everything a country house needed, from a double garage and built-in oak settles to a view of the South Downs.

Jo had visited him there and they had had some happy times before the bombs and everything else intervened, so they decided to use the name at Iffley. For this house, of course, Ken could only achieve a 'second-hand' description, as seen through other eyes and felt for himself. An eighty-foot frontage, 'bags of basins' in the four bedrooms, and a dining-room with a stove. They used the breakfast room also as a kitchen, because Sandra had the kitchen as a 'dog room!' Ken always remembers staircases clearly, and this one ran up sideways from the square hall.

They had to be careful when buying houses to avoid those 'insignificant' little steps up and down which could be such a perpetual nuisance to a blind person. And 'ye olde worlde' timbers about 5¾ feet above floor-level were always out. No steps, or Ken would twist an ankle; no low doors or ceilings, or he would hit his head.

The half-acre of garden at Mallows was really rather much, and eventually proved too much, for Jo to manage. But in 1955 they still enjoyed all the pleasant spaciousness of the place after the cramped semi-detached at Cowley.

The first time Ken and Sandra set off for Iffley Village Hall, she seemed to find it by herself. It was quite uncanny how she seemed to know where Ken wanted to go, and on this occasion, she heard a record playing and turned straight into the entrance to the village hall without his having to ask anyone the way at all. Other times Ken would take Sandra for an evening walk free of her harness and lead, after he had learned the way down a gentle 400-yard slope near the house.

A specially chartered coach took the Oxford team to Harrogate in November 1955, which was to be the origin of the *Top Town* contest against Cambridge. All the team, including Sandra, spent the night at the Valley Hotel, Harrogate, and were up early next morning to rehearse for the actual show. Ken came to grips for the first time with the expectant sounds of a television studio as men clattered about, and the odd strains of an introduction to a song was heard. All day they rehearsed until the last break before the evening transmission, and then in a flash it seemed they were on the air. One minute forty seconds. That was how long he had. One hundred seconds.

The floor manager said, "Quiet, everyone."

A hush, and then: "O.K. Announcement on." Another tense moment, and then the crash of the band opening the show. This faded for their own announcer at Harrogate, Peter Haigh, to introduce the contest and launch each team into the show. Ten acts in twenty minutes, the total time for each team.

The show had started with a picture first of Oxford – Magdalen Bridge and the town – then of a Cambridge college. But it was Cambridge who went in first. Twenty minutes later it was Oxford and a students' song about the city famous for marmalade and traffic jams! Tap dancing, bones played as scissors, a song or two, and then Ken's turn came closer.

Ken could not expect any prompting as to the right time to start his song, since the team's show ran non-stop. A comedy act, and then he had to be prepared. At the last chord of the act ahead of him, he squatted down on his haunches. He wanted to leave this as late as possible, for it was not a comfortable singing position.

Ken heard the last chord, followed by an *arpeggio*, and he had to assume that the cameras were panning around to him. He had to stay on his spot rigidly, and be sure to keep Sandra by his side. She did not stir. And almost without his realizing it, Alyn Ainsworth and the Northern Dance Orchestra had played their accompaniment and he had sung his song, or her song. It was all over, and soon Oxford came to their finale.

When both teams had finished the last three minutes of the programme generated an unbearable state of tension. All eyes turned towards the three judges. All except Ken's. Peter Haigh introduced Jack Train, Dorothy Ward, and Ted Kavanagh, and then asked for their verdict.

Dorothy Ward said she thought that both teams would provide an intimate West End review, "but I think I must say Oxford has it." Ted Kavanagh liked a lot of things the Cambridge team did, "but for novelty, originality, fluency, and polish, I must give my verdict to Oxford." And Jack Train concluded: "Cambridge were marvellous; Oxford more than marvellous. Oxford are the winners." Ken heard the magic name "Oxford," and roared out with the rest of the team. They had won.

Ken was back on television a month later. The B.B.C. picked leading acts from all the previous programmes and presented a *Top Town Parade* on Boxing Night from Lime Grove studios. They asked Ken to appear, to sing a song and be interviewed. So, Ken and Jo and Sandra headed for London that Christmas.

Once again Sandra was part of the act, and once again nearly stole it by eating a bit of biscuit. Peter Haigh asked Ken about his experiences. Ken revealed that since his accident he had survived no less than twenty plastic operations of one sort and another. When Haigh asked about hobbies, he mentioned dancing and going out with the beagles, which he did by the device of holding on to someone with one end of a walking stick.

He dedicated his song *Please* to Jo, who was there, as he put it, "when they carried in the pieces to East Grinstead," and had been there ever since.

In a further *Top Town* series the following summer at Manchester, Oxford competed against Douglas, Isle of Man, and Ken sang *Who are we?* But this time Oxford were less lucky, and lost.

Ken has always liked good jazz and has a collection of records, including some early "Jelly Roll" Morton and other artists. He admires traditionalists like Chris Barber and Acker Bilk, but best of all he feels an affinity to the music of George Shearing, the brilliant blind jazz pianist who went to America from Britain. So, Ken is not content to stay in the rut he could so easily have found for himself. Instead, he lives as fully as anyone – more so than many people. And his life is changing, expanding, all the time.

Ken and Jo were both learning the do's and don'ts of being blind. She saw that the furniture was never moved around without telling him, but kept it in the same spot so that Ken could always get his bearings easily. Nor did she leave stray things lying about that he might trip over. Doors were left either tightly shut or wide open flat against the wall. Half-open doors are a menace to those who are blind. Similarly with cupboards. They were finding the convenience to Ken of sliding doors and cupboards, and fitting these as they could afford to do so.

As he grew older, too, Ken's sense of humour seemed to be developing, and he would see the funny side of irritating things. A friend sitting down to a meal with him sometimes waited till he had forked some food into his mouth and nearly swallowed it before announcing, "That's a sausage, Ken."

"Go on! Is it really?"

A well-meaning canteen girl leaned over him intimately one midday and said, "I've taken the stones out of your prunes, Mr Revis."

"Thank you," answered Ken graciously, "but it's my sight that's gone – not my tongue!"

Yet whatever life involved now, Sandra seemed an inseparable part of it. For eight years she guided Ken faithfully, and two more years she kept him company. Then for several weeks she started to fail. She went off her food, moped, and showed no excitement at anything. Usually, she was dancing around all the time, and Ken grew almost unconsciously aware of the thump of her feet up and down on the lino of the floors at Mallows. When he mentioned a walk to her, she normally fetched his stick for him to stroll down the slope in the evening. Now she did not bother about things, and they knew that something was wrong. This was the terrible time for anyone with a dog. For Ken it was worse.

They drove her to the vet, and she lay unduly still in the back seat.

"Her liver's not working well," Miss Ballard said. "I'll give her some pills, but I can't say how much good they will do."

The pills helped for a while, but she never seemed lively, and they missed her dancing on her hind-legs in excitement. Her legs seemed affected as well. The listlessness returned, and Ken and Jo tried the vet again. Miss Ballard gave her an injection this time as well as the pills, as a strange air settled over the house that Christmas.

"I hope this isn't going to be the end – but I'm afraid it may be," Ken said somehow.

"I'll do all I can." Miss Ballard knew how much Sandra meant to both of them.

Each day, when Ken came home, the first question and answer was, "How is she?"

"No better, Ken."

It reached the stage when Sandra could not walk out into the garden. She could only just about stand and sway. Each time she wanted to go outside, Ken gathered her up around her legs, taking care not to hurt her stomach, and stayed with her on the lawn till she was ready to be brought indoors again to her bed in the breakfast-room. She was losing weight regularly each day. Finally, Ken said, "If she's no better to-morrow I'll have to get the vet."

Jo could not risk speaking.

Next morning Sandra was reasonably comfortable, but could not eat or get up. Her tail had not wagged for weeks now.

Ken phoned Miss Ballard. "I think you'd better come. I don't think there's much hope with Sandra."

He went back into the breakfast-room weeping. He said his own good-bye to her. Jo was crying too. Half an hour later the vet rang the bell.

Jo said, "I'm going upstairs, Ken. I can't stay down here."

Miss Ballard saw Ken was having a hard time to stand it. He was still weeping as she shaved the fur off a patch of Sandra's paw. Ken held the paw still with his thumb, stroking it slightly. The vet gave Sandra the injection, and Ken felt her head fall to one side.

"Is that all?" he gulped.

"Yes. I'll get my car."

Miss Ballard backed the car up to the front door, opened the boot softly, and between them they lifted Sandra and laid her inside. As the engine faded into the distance, Ken shivered in the January air and turned to find Jo, still upstairs. It was one of the worst days of their lives.

143

Chapter 10

AN AMBITION ACHIEVED

Next to Jo, her sister Jane is probably the person closest to Ken, and for five years, from 1954, she helped him invaluably to fulfil a fresh ambition. Jane's memory of Ken goes back to 1939, however, when she used to hide behind the settee as a small girl, and then surprise Ken and Jo when they were sitting on it!

The days following his accident are still vivid to her. She remembers the telegram, her mother rushing out to the nearest phone-box to tell her father, and the Yorkshire pudding left to spoil in the oven. She walked over to Ken's bed on the right-hand side of the ward, and was shocked to see the bandages across his eyes.

Ken said quietly, "Hello, Janet." That was before she dropped the 't.' She had an urge to cry, but did not. Jo was acting comparatively normally in the circumstances. The family were amazed at her spirit. A Canadian with a canopy over his bed gave Jane some sweets, and she visited Ken several times while she was down at East Grinstead.

Jane's father retired in 1950, and they planned to move to the Oxford area to be near Ken and Jo, but the housing situation proved so impossible that they had to modify this scheme. The nearest convenient house they could find was just outside Reading, so Ken and Jo suggested that while Jane was at school in Oxford, she should live with them. These years in Jane's middle 'teens developed her attachment to Ken and Jo, although she did not always see eye to eye with them. Occasionally they would feel the weight of their 'parental' responsibility towards her and be a bit strict, but on the whole the three of them got on amazingly well.

At the end of the day, a little ritual would be for Jane to go into their room, sit on the bed, and chat over the day's happenings and any particular problems. Ken helped her with her homework frequently, and he evolved a way of turning names round to make them

144

sound funny. This seemed a natural thing for Ken to concentrate on verbal humour, and he has now a keen sense of the absurd. Even then, though, Jane recalls him as behaving almost as a sighted person by showing some one around their room and asking, for example, "Do you like this vase?"

The trio used to gang up in different groupings, too. Ken and Jo to restrain Jane's youthful extremes; Jo and Jane to wear Ken down into buying something Jo wanted; and Ken and Jane to play some trick on Jo. Jane was increasingly interested in dramatic art and stage make-up, and took a lot of teasing from Ken about it. But he kept so straight-faced that she could not be sure when he was serious or otherwise. After leaving school, Jane wanted to go on to the stage, but realized she was not ideally cut out for it despite the dazzling features she had developed, so took a job with a beauty and hair salon. And by now she was bringing boy-friends home to Ken and Jo.

About this period, too, Ken was beginning to find that he had too much time on his hands at the office, time to dwell on how his life was shaping. This began to prey on him a bit, and early in 1954 the idea suddenly came to him that he had to do something more to prove himself, or he would slip into this permanent rut and it would be too late. Sensibly, he always appreciated his limitations as well as his abilities – in other words, what could and what could not be done – and he began to go through the various professions to try and find one for which he could qualify.

"A lawyer. That's it. That's what I'll be."

He was quite sure in his mind, but he knew absolutely nothing about the law, and, in fact, exactly what *kind* of a lawyer he meant to become. He did not even know the real difference between a barrister and a solicitor.

Ken went to see Reginald Hanks, the vice-chairman of the Nuffield Organization, to discuss the question.

"Will you release me to qualify as a lawyer?" Ken asked him.

The vice-chairman was very nice about it, but suggested that first Ken went away and found out precisely what the training entailed, and then came back for a further talk. Once Ken has made up his mind, nothing deflects or delays him, so he was soon talking to Rupert Cross, the blind senior law tutor at Magdalen College, Oxford, about his plan. The two men sat on opposite sides of a desk in the don's study, neither able to see the other.

"Well, if you want to be a solicitor you'll have to be articled, of course," Cross told Ken.

"All right. I'll try that."

Cross himself had qualified not only as a solicitor, but a barrister, too, and he had a law degree.

Back at home again Ken asked Jo, "Now, who do we know as a solicitor?" Then they remembered Charles Gilman. When they had been prosecuted for a parking offence in Oxford Gilman had defended them, acting on behalf of the R.A.C. Once more Ken acted immediately and rang up Gilman.

"Can I come and see you?"

Gilman agreed, and Ken and Jo found themselves in the offices of Marshall and Eldridge. Ken went in to see Gilman alone, and reminded him of the parking episode before sketching his whole history to the solicitor in less than five minutes. Then Ken came straight to the point.

"I'm wondering if you'll consider having me as an articled clerk?"

"Why, yes, of course."

There was no delay in Gilman's acceptance, although he had never before contemplated the implications – and complications – of having a blind articled clerk. He buzzed for Jo to come up and be introduced, and it was all settled so quickly that Ken hardly had time himself to realize what was happening.

When Ken returned to the vice-chairman and told him, he got a characteristically understanding reception.

"All right. We'll give you the time off to qualify. And we'd like you to come back and work with us afterwards, but we won't hold you to it."

In fact, although being articled and studying was a full-time job, Ken did continue giving the induction talks at the factory for several months more.

"Would you like to be my secretary?" Ken asked Jane, when he got home after arranging everything with the solicitors. She did not need asking again, and the two of them arrived at the office on the very first morning, to be greeted with a pile of deeds and other documents and a mass of instructions. Neither Ken nor Jane knew a thing about the law, and they gasped as they were left alone with all this fearsome-looking paraphernalia. Luckily the other articled clerk, Frank Barrington-Ward, helped out. And when Ken and Jane had to take some of them round to another firm of solicitors, the qualified man there fortunately knew what was wanted.

"You'll need a memorandum," he said.

"Thanks very much," agreed Ken.

That first week, Ken drafted his own articles of clerkship, which were dated 2 June 1954, with its references to zealous and sober behaviour, and agreement not to deface the books or articles of his master. There was a modified attestation clause used in the case of blind persons.

"You've got to read it and read it and read it," Barrington-Ward told Ken straight away, as they discussed studying, but the basic obstacle was that Ken had to be read to by someone else at first, until he developed other more cunning techniques. So, Barrington-Ward, or Barry, and Jane started off that first week on Stephen's *Commentaries on the Laws of England*, the standard set of textbooks for beginners.

Before launching into this new profession, Ken had been to see Lady Fraser at St Dunstan's to tell her about his aim. She agreed to help by paying for his textbooks and some extras, including assistance with accommodation later in London, and also Jane's salary.

So, the five-year plan got under way. Ken and Jane went around together everywhere, on completion of house purchase and all the other legal work of a busy solicitor's office. One of the statutory obligations undertaken by articles is attendance at the Law Society's School of Law or at a approved establishment such as the Faculty of Law, Oxford University. Ken could enrol for this, fortunately, and did so promptly, indicating his intention to take his Intermediate Examination in 1956. The subjects in this exam came under three papers: (1) real property; (2) contract and tort; (3) criminal law and evidence; constitutional law; courts of justice. Ken had to go to different Oxford colleges for each of these subjects: to Keble for real property, Balliol for contract, and so on.

"There's an awfully nice-looking boy who smiles at me," Jane whispered to Ken during a lull in the first lecture at Keble College. Ken chuckled and made some suitable retort. Ken and Jane always sat fairly close together at lectures to discuss any point in the notes, and usually occupied one of the front benches for Ken to hear as clearly as he could. Jane made her 'longhand-shorthand' notes on one of the bare wooden tables in front of each bench.

John Martyn had first noticed Jane with Ken as they were turning into Balliol for one of the first lectures of the Michaelmas Term, and felt suddenly: What an attractive girl! but he did not expect to see her again. Then when she turned up at Keble with Ken it seemed too good to be true, yet there was little he could do about it. Whenever he saw them, their arms were linked. Ken likes to walk about half a pace behind a guide, though there are some people who push him in front in a way that really alarms him and frequently results in collisions. John Martyn did not realize at first that Ken was blind at all, and thought Jane had her arm through his, instead of the other way round. Even when it did dawn on him that she was guiding him, there was still no way of knowing whether or not she was a student, or what relationship existed between the two of them. He could not understand why Jane should return his smile yet seem so attached to Ken!

A couple of weeks passed before John actually said, "Hello" to them, and another little while till he came and sat with them at lectures. Now he really looked forward to the Tuesday lectures, when he could be sure of seeing Jane. The three of them went on like this for most of the Michaelmas Term. By then it was time for feminine wiles to break the deadlock, and Jane explained to Jo how she liked the look of John very much, but Ken was always there. "The old ogre," as Ken described himself.

At the next lecture, Ken asked as many questions about the subject as usual while Jane scribbled away at the notes. John sat patiently alongside, and then the three of them trooped out to the gates of the college. That was as far as John could get, without appearing presumptuous. But on this day, according to a prearranged plan, Jo was waiting outside in the car. John had actually dropped behind.

"Hello. I've come to pick you up to take you to the hairdressers, Ken, and then there's that fitting for your sports coat." Ken was always particular about his clothes and general appearance. With that, Ken groped for the car door, opened it, and got in.

"Cheerio," Jo called as she let in the clutch.

John caught Jane up and asked her to walk down the road with him. So, in a few minutes the situation was explained to him, and they had arranged to go to the new Oxford Union Club. This little cavern of a jazz club had been built in some cleared cellars, and was ideal for drinking and dancing. Lady Docker opened it earlier in the year, and, like everyone else, fell for its unusual decor and murals. There had been nothing like it at the University before, and Ken and Jo later made a foursome with John and Jane several times. Ken's dancing was as smooth as ever, with a strong sense of rhythm. Over the next few years, they noticed the deterioration in dress at the club from dinner jackets to lounge suits, and then to open necks! Still, it was always a good spot for a couple of pints of college ale.

Meanwhile Ken and Jane grew steadily closer, and he asked her the sort of things that he would previously only put to Jo. He has always been very interested in what people look like, and Jo tries to liken them to film-stars or other faces that Ken knew when he could see. Jo had also by this time developed the habit of always telling him about clothes or furnishings or anything she bought, describing their shade and style. Ken could then feel the particular thing and get to know it. He appreciates this, and also likes the way Jo drives. She makes sure, too, of remembering that Ken likes to order the wine they occasionally have, and pay the bill himself.

Now Ken began to ask Jane such things as, "How much grey hair have I got?"

"Just a few up here," she said, touching his temples.

"And tell me truthfully, Jane, what's the old face like nowadays?"

"It's very nice, Ken. The scars have merged in well and weathered wonderfully."

Which is quite true, although he will always bear some signs of that instant of time at Brighton, after which he was not expected to live.

Not only can Ken never know what he looks like now, he cannot really know exactly how Jo has matured, and Jane he has never seen since she was a little girl.

Jane learned a lot about Ken and his ways. He had a very characteristic style of swinging into the creaking office, and this confident approach into any rooms he knew was one of the things she admired him for so much. Then, as now, Ken liked to have vivacious people with him if possible – probably one of the reasons why he got on so well with Jane, who had grown into the same sort of lively girl as Jo. And because of this very liveliness they clashed at times about some things. Ken is a sensitive person, yet not deeply involved in the arts, perhaps inevitably, since he is bound to miss a certain amount of appreciation. They used to have riotous arguments about the right attitude to the arts, with Ken irked at times with the B.B.C. radio programme of *The Critics* broadcast on Sundays.

But apart from everything else, Ken and Jane had the law to bind them together over these years of the mid-fifties. She never knew she would become such an authority on such an unlikely subject as tort. Ken gradually found that the lectures, although interesting, could not really be as valuable to someone like himself taking the Law Society examinations as to an undergraduate reading the theory of law. The Law Society's approach was inevitably much more practical, less remote. And there was one famous lecture on constitutional law when they sat at the back of a large hall and hardly heard a single word!

To and from lectures and the office, Ken and Jane became well-known figures in the city, and she found that people still stared quite directly at them often. She had a special sign of squeezing his arm, which meant that they were about to step down or up a kerb. The only snag from Jane's point of view was that she had to remember to switch off her guiding role when she went out with John, which she did more and more since that delayed first real meeting.

Jane read all the standard textbooks to Ken two or three times, and Barrington-Ward was also helpful in this way. Once, in the office, Ken had dictated a letter to Jane while making a conveyance, and Barry had offered to read to him for a while. It was hot in the room, and as Barry's voice went on Ken nodded off to sleep lightly. Jane at once noticed this and made a point of getting up and reaching across his desk, apparently for an envelope, but, in fact, to waken him without Barry knowing. Another day, Jane actually fell asleep while reading to Ken!

Ken was lucky, too, to get several local people from Iffley to come in and read out loud to him. Three women and two men helped him in this way, and it was at this stage that he began to realize what an aid his tape-recorder could be. He did not always feel like being read to at the precise time people could manage, so in this way he could please himself a little. He switched on his recorder to hear them initially – or Jane when she could manage it as well – and then he was able to play it back whenever he felt like it. Early mornings were a good time for this, an hour which he would otherwise have had to waste.

Jane started to tape-record her notes of the lectures, too, and these would be occasionally interspersed with such recorded comments as, "Damn, I forgot to get that shampoo!"

Another aid to Ken was something he believed to be unique. When learning law, the student is always coming up against unfamiliar terms, both English and Latin. To explain these Osborn's *A Concise Law Dictionary*, actually almost an encyclopaedia, is invaluable, but Ken could not refer to it without asking someone to look up the particular point each time. He approached St Dunstan's, therefore, who agreed to have it put into braille for him. This was another 'special' job, rather like the Oriental one done for his Indian appointment. The dictionary was transcribed on to braille sheets, which were then bound into some ten volumes. The whole work was undertaken by arrangement with the National Institute for the Blind. When it was ready, Ken had at his disposal a braille version of the latest edition of this useful reference book, containing every word and term connected with the law. "Felony," for instance, did not merely define the word but list and describe many of the more important cases to illustrate it. And vital, too, to Ken were the reminders of the exact meanings of all the Latin 'tags' used in law: *inter alia, sine die*, etc.

Ken got on so well with Jane's help that he decided he would be ready to take the Intermediate Examination in July 1956, just over two years after entering into his articles. This meant a move to London to attend the course at the Law Society's School of Law, which was due to commence on 5 January.

Jo drove Ken up there before Christmas to find some suitable accommodation for him, and they settled on a small place, Carmel House Hotel, which was conveniently close to the School of Law's address at Lancaster Gate. The hotel consisted of a couple of tall Victorian houses which had been knocked into one, and the manager assured Jo that he would look after Ken well.

The next problem was personal help with his studies. Jane could not come up to London, but Ken was lucky to find an equally good replacement.

Ken had met the Countess of Bandon some time before at a Guide Dogs Ball held at the Mayfair Hotel in London. Sandra did her collecting act on this occasion with the aid of a wickerwork basket strapped to her back, and the whole evening helped the Guide Dogs fund by a large sum.

Later on, the Countess brought her daughter, Lady Jennifer Bernard, to a little cocktail-party at Mallows, where Ken met her for the first time. She told him she was between jobs at that moment, and as he felt she had the right mixture of patience and understanding, Ken asked her if she would accept the job of his assistant. The dark-haired debutante accepted.

Ken and Jo felt rather sad on that first evening at Carmel House before she left him there. Although he would get home most week-ends, this marked their first real series of separations since the early days at St Dunstan's in 1944, apart from his operations. But they cheered up when they discovered that there were at least a couple of other law students staying at the same hotel. They met one of them on the spiral staircase that evening.

"We make coffee in the evening," he told Ken. "You must come into my room for it with the other chap."

So, the routine got going. Jennifer left her Chelsea flat each morning, met Ken at his Bayswater hotel, and took him to the School of Law for the morning lectures from 10.30 till 1. She soon learned to make notes of exactly what he wanted. Then, after lunch at the canteen amid the clatter of dozens of other articled clerks on the course, they went back to Carmel House to mug up the morning's work. Jennifer read back his notes to him, prepared him for the following day's lectures, and checked any legal references he needed from the library.

Colin Glynne-Jones, the student on the stairs, read to Ken as well, or else they tested each other with questions and answers. Brian Frost, the other student, was also very helpful to him. Ken's tape-recorder really repaid its cost now, as Jennifer and Brian both read a lot on to it for him to play back in the evenings. One or two of the ladies in the hotel also offered to read his textbooks, so he did not suffer from lack of helpers. A favourite form of study for Ken was to turn his tape-recorder on in bed and listen to it in real comfort.

Although Jennifer acted as guide and general help, Ken kept as independent as he could. He washed his socks and pants whenever necessary, and an occasional nylon shirt. A jam jar full of "Daz" became one of his best friends for these operations. He had a gas-ring in the room, where he made coffee for himself and the others, and as the winter passed, he always kept plenty of fresh fruit there for snacks while studying. Colin often made the tea or coffee in his own room or else over the ring in Ken's.

Word soon passed around Carmel House about Ken, and he got to know all the residents there – except one. They usually reserved an armchair near the door for Ken to use, but a deaf old colonel staying there was not aware of this arrangement and sat there one day. The colonel had hardly settled himself down before Ken came into the room, and, with his usual methodical manner, made straight for his chair. He tried to sit down and felt himself squarely on the colonel's lap. The colonel, for some reason, would not have it that Ken could not see, and seemed to regard him as crazy.

Anyway, the old man made a rapid exit as if his life depended on it. The next unlucky occasion came when the colonel was on his way up to his room one evening. He found the stairs rather tiring, and had the habit of resting half-way, on the bottom step of one of the flights. The colonel perched on his accustomed tread, facing downstairs, just as Ken came careering two at a time down the flight and knocked him flying! Ken could not see; the colonel could not hear: that was the dilemma.

But the colonel refused to try to make contact with Ken, who called out loudly, "Sorry, colonel, are you all right?"

The old man did not say a word, but just grabbed the banister and fled on upstairs.

Another day when Ken was sitting in his armchair with his braille books placed as usual on the mantelpiece within reach, an elderly spinster came in and sat beside him.

"What are those things up there?" she asked.

"Oh, they're braille books."

"There must be a blind lady in the hotel somewhere, mustn't there?"

But before Ken could grapple with this situation, the dinner-bell sounded and she trotted in to her meal. Later on, however, she returned to the same spot in the lounge and started talking to Ken once more. The conversation turned to holiday places, and particularly Monte Carlo.

"I've been there, you know. I've got a brochure in my bag about it. Here it is. Look – that's the hotel where I was. And there's the beach just beside it."

"How lovely!" Ken commented.

She rambled on for quite a while, pointing out to him all the various sights she remembered, and Ken kept up the pretence of seeing the brochure. His eyes must be better than he realized!

So, this time had its lighter moments to relieve the strain of study. There was Miss McClelland who hung packets of digestive biscuits on the door of his room as a little surprise for him! He would come upon these little offerings as he felt for the handle. By now, Ken had complete control of the complicated route from his room, along corridors, down the stairs, to the lounge and dining-room.

After the summer holiday they returned to the school with only a month to go. They had had a test at the end of each subject by this stage.

"Below 40 per cent, you'll never pass," Ken had heard. So, he felt quite pleased with 56 per cent, for one test, and the fact that his lowest mark was 41 per cent, on property. Despite the comfort of this, the work and the tension built up during these final few weeks. At last, the days came: 5 and 6 July. Morning, afternoon, and morning.

He felt fortunate at being examined in the same building where he had been attending, as strange surroundings made a lot of difference when there is no time to get acclimatized to them. There were the little details like finding out where the toilets were situated, and similar endless queries. At Lancaster Gate, Ken could use the same canteen and feel familiar with things generally. Jennifer got him there in good time, and he was shown into the allotted room, where he met the lady invigilator. She seemed friendly and assured him she had done this before. They arranged themselves at right angles along the end of a table, and then the first sealed envelope was brought in formally. Its bearer said, "All right, Mr Revis, it's coming up to 10.30 now, so go ahead and good luck."

The invigilator asked Ken how he would like the paper read, and he told her that he would like to hear the whole paper first, before re-reading individual questions. The first three questions were compulsory, and then he had to attempt seven out of the next nine: a total of ten. When they got down to each question, she read it once or twice till he knew it. Then Ken dictated the answers, which she took down in longhand; sometimes he amended a sentence before being satisfied. There were no serious snags, and Ken completed the examination moderately pleased.

Back in Oxford with Marshall and Eldridge for a couple of months, he awaited the day of the results. He learned that if he phoned the secretary of the principal on 6 August, he would hear how it had gone. John Martyn was helping Ken in the office and elsewhere during the summer vacation from University, and the two of them were in the office together as Ken rang through to London.

153

"Hello, it's Revis speaking . . ."

Ken did not get any farther before the secretary at the other end interrupted him, "Oh, yes, you're through all right, Mr Revis."

They whooped for joy and at once broke the good news to Jo and Jane. That was half the battle over – or almost. The other detail: to take trust accounts and book-keeping, the subsidiary part of the Intermediate.

This course occupied only two days a week, so for the rest of the time Ken went to the office of his solicitors' London agents. This entailed travelling by tube from Lancaster Gate to the Bank, and then via the Royal Exchange and Threadneedle Street to Old Broad Street. Ken hated the noise and the rush hour, but for four months he stuck it out as "something – but not very much – in the City." He attended county courts and the High Court, with solicitors and managing clerks, and generally learned what London meant to a lawyer. Then came the exam at the end of November.

Ken is extremely good at mental arithmetic, and this helped him in these subjects, as it did also in reckoning rent apportionments and other intricacies involving money matters in the law. He took the exam orally, as he could not be expected to write or work out double-entry book-keeping and similar things on paper. The examiner was very kind in his attitude towards Ken, offering cigarettes and sweets, but the exam itself was, of course, exactly the same as other students were sitting. He passed it. That really was half-way.

London had been an experience, including outings to the Humphrey Lyttelton jazz club, but Ken was very relieved to return to the comparative quiet of Oxford again to resume his work. The year 1957 was marked by a wonderful Majorca holiday, and marred at Christmas by the illness of Sandra. Only a fortnight after Sandra died, the phone rang at Iffley one morning. It was Jo's mother.

"It's Daddy. He's died in the night."

Ken broke it to Jo – as Jane came running downstairs asking, "What's the matter?"

It was a terrible blow to the two girls, who had worshipped their father. He was a youthful seventy-two, and they had never seriously considered this happening for years yet.

John and Jane had planned to be married in March, and it was decided by the family as a whole not to postpone the wedding because of this loss. Mr Smith had been going to give Jane away; now Ken was next in line. He also undertook quite a lot of the actual arrangements for the ceremony at St Michael's-in-the-Northgate, Oxford, including such inevitable details as photographers. He also had to phone frantically for the bride's car, which had not arrived some while after the time due. Eventually it came, and they set out for the church.

It was just as well they had been delayed, for while John and his brother Arthur were waiting at the church with all the other guests, they suddenly heard a peculiar noise behind them. Turning round they saw a strange little man dressed in oilskins, boots, and spectacles, carrying a pile of books, trundling up the aisle! When he reached the top of the aisle, oblivious to everything, he put down the books and went on to his knees to pray. John and Arthur coughed several times without effect, and then eventually Arthur tapped the man on the shoulder softly, whereupon he got up quite unconcerned and retraced his way.

At that moment, Ken was handing Jane out of the car outside the church, and Ken, in full morning dress, appeared to be leading her up the aisle, whereas, in fact, she was guiding him! They stopped before the altar, and Ken handed Jane forward. Jo then tapped his shoulder and guided him to the front pew next to her. Afterwards came the pictures and reception at Mallows, which Jo had decorated specially for her sister. Ken made one of the speeches.

For some time before this Ken had been experiencing increasing difficulty with his breathing. He paid regular visits to the Radcliffe Hospital, where he had various nose drops and electric cauterizing treatment. The latter went right up his nose and was very unpleasant. Eventually, when it seemed to get no better, he was told, "It wouldn't be a bad idea if you went up to the Churchill for an operation."

So, he was admitted into this hospital for a week or so, and operated on for about the twentieth time – he had lost exact count by now. They cut a hole in the passage at the back of the nose to relieve this congested breathing, and after some weeks of settling down, it did definitely improve. Ken still has a certain soreness if the nose gets dry and hardens. If it does, he uses some "Vaseline" to ease it, but the main thing is for him to avoid very dry air. Electric fires irritate his nose more than central heating, while open coal fires are best of all. As well as this periodic irritation, Ken also has strong singing noises in his head at times, another legacy of his accident.

With the summer Ken started his Finals course at the School of Law, with Jane once more as his secretary. This was soon broken up by a month's holiday in Paris and Italy, and then came the six months' sweat. Jane was recording a lot of material on tape now, and he also managed to get several of the lecturers to record various of their compressed notes for him. These were the equivalent of the sighted students' full copies of the notes which they were always given. The snag was that on tape there was no flicking back a page or two to check a point, though

Ken really did get his tapes filed so precisely that he could turn one up almost as quickly as opening a book. Some fifty tapes in all – and he knew where each one was placed.

Jane read the notes to him on the balcony of his bedroom till about five o'clock every day, and then she would leave him. She felt somehow sad to go, as she saw him sitting there alone with only his tapes and braille dictionary. She knew too well that unless someone happened to ask him out, he could not get away from the hotel. The same sort of feeling must have crept over Ken, too, for he began to sleep very badly throughout these last months to the Finals. The course was tougher, and he had to take sleeping-pills all the time. Another worry for him was the ignorance of the standard required to get through the exam, and so he started to sit up every night with his tapes, with too few week-end breaks. He was working far too hard, and he knew in his own mind that he must be not far off a nervous breakdown. Jane did what she could by taking his mind off things with news of the latest fashions – the sack, pointed shoes, and so on – but he did not improve.

Jo went down to stay at Carmel House during the exam, and as soon as she saw Ken on that day in March 1959, she knew he shouldn't be taking it. He was usually so good at distinguishing people's voices, but now he began to make mistakes, and not be able to tell from which part of the room they were coming. By the time he actually sat for the exam he was pretty groggy, and could not string words together properly after the seven-hour days of answering questions. As soon as it was over, Jo took him home to Oxford, where the doctor ordered him to bed at once for two weeks.

"You've got to rest completely, Mr Revis, and not think of the future or anything. Just relax. You've been overdoing it for a long time."

Even after he was up and about again, Ken could not make the effort of listening to the radio or television, and even simple questions in panel games floored him completely. It took him the whole month of waiting for the results before he felt much better. Then he heard what he had expected: passes in only three of the seven subjects.

He had learned his lesson, however, and determined to be more sensible next time.

John and Jane were settled in a flat in Bayswater by May 1959 and so Ken took a room in a house next door. And just as his articles expired, he started a course with the commercial firm of Gibson and Weldon to prepare for the Finals again in November. On the anniversary of his articles, he wrote and thanked Charles Gilman for all he had done to help, and then Ken got down to it.

Ken's room was on the second floor of the house, and after he had got up, washed, shaved, and dressed, he made his way down to the pavement, felt a route along the front railings past prams and other obstructions, and then descended the steps to John and Jane in their lower ground-floor flat for breakfast. Jane escorted him to Chancery Lane for lectures, and later took down his dictated answers to the various tests held regularly.

He felt far better with Gibson and Weldon, and restrained himself from doing too much. Together they prepared for November sensibly, including the technique of getting used to comprehending questions after only one or two hearings. One of the previous troubles had been that in his tense state, Ken had become confused by having to try to sort out six-part questions in his head and then dictate answers logically.

The Finals arrived, and he took them in the hall of the Law Society. His invigilator was a retired schoolmaster, who sat with him in a room separate from the main body of students. An early light moment occurred when Ken dictated the word "sodomy."

"Have you really got to use terms like that?" the invigilator asked.

The whole operation was almost military in its planning. John, Jane, and Jo all packed up great baskets of food for lunches during the exam, which ran for three and a half days non-stop: 24½ hours of it for Ken. They cooked steaks in advance, and brought with them salads, fruit, and bottles of milk for John and Ken to eat in the building itself before going for a walk around Lincoln's Inn Fields.

The seven subjects were: real property and conveyancing; contract and tort; equity and succession; divorce and private international law; commercial law; income tax, estate duty, stamp duty; company law and partnership.

As Ken ploughed on through these interminable papers, Jo and Jane often got to the Law Society a while before he was due to finish. The two sisters sat on the steps by the lift, just outside the room where Ken was intoning away his answers, which they could hear quite distinctly.

"Gosh, I hope he's remembered that case," Jane exploded as she strained her ears to catch a part of one question and then his answer. John felt just as strongly about the outcome, too, and they all waited there right up to the last minute. Often Ken would be looking at his braille watch and muttering, "Five more minutes, and another part of the question still to go."

Jane had played the tapes back to him so often they had almost worn the recorder out. Now their work was paying off, as Ken came to the end of the last paper. Five and a half years of slogging.

A month later, Ken and Jo were in the Royal Restaurant, Liverpool, after a drizzling wet winter day. He was feeling tense as he waited for the Finals results the following day. Then, quite unexpectedly, they met someone from the City desk of a Liverpool paper, who told them that there might be a chance of getting the results sooner.

Unknown to Ken, their companion, Bill Scott-Comber, left them about midnight and rang the paper. The early editions were going to press, and he asked, "Can you tell me if K.C. Revis has passed the Law Society Finals, please?"

After a pause, the answer came back, "Yes."

"Are you sure? Will you spell it back to me?"

Scott-Comber walked back to their table, gave a thumbs-up sign to Jo, and laid his hand on Ken's shoulder.

"Congratulations, Ken, you've passed."

Some time afterwards Ken received the following official admission:

> In the Supreme Court:
> Whereas, upon Examination and Enquiry touching the fitness and capacity of Kenneth Claude Revis, M.B.E., of Little Mallows, 23 Capel Close, Oxford, to act as a Solicitor of the Supreme Court, I am satisfied that the said Kenneth Claude Revis is a fit and proper person so to act.
>
> I do by this writing under my hand Admit the said Kenneth Claude Revis to be a Solicitor of the Supreme Court.
>
> Dated this first day of March 1960.
>
> *(Signed)* M.R. Evershed
> T. Lund
> Secretaries to the Law Society.
> Enrolled 1st March 1960.

Ken answered the question of why he wanted to become a solicitor in this simple way: "It was largely a personal challenge."

Then he rejoined the British Motor Corporation as an assistant Press officer to start a new phase of his life.

Chapter 11

100 M.P.H. WITHOUT EYES

But while Ken was still studying the law in the summer of 1958, his life took yet another turn, which later indirectly enabled him to fulfil his greatest ambition since being blinded.

His achievements had been helped by a number of people, apart from the parents on both sides. First of all, Jo had been there all the time. Then there was Sandra, not strictly a person, but just as important to Ken. Next came Jane with her rare blend of youth plus patience. And after the *Top Town* era, Billy Scott-Comber, who later broke the news of his Finals pass, became a close friend of both Ken and Jo.

This engaging Irishman sang with Jack Payne and his band for ten years before the war, later topped the bill all over the country with his singing Grenadiers, and made altogether some two thousand gramophone records. But he was far from being just another singer. He had the background of five years at the Abbey Theatre, Dublin, as well as friendships with many of the leading Irish theatrical personalities, such as Barry Fitzgerald and Noel Purcell, the poet W.B. Yeats, and, more recently, colourful characters like Brendan Behan. Scott-Comber wrote a number of hit songs including *With me shillelagh under me arm* and *Here's to the hills and here's to the heather*. The latter one in praise of Scotland did remarkably well until someone revealed that its composer was an Irishman!

In 1958 he was still a contract producer for B.B.C. Northern Region based in Manchester, and travelling thousands of miles a year in his work. He had contacts with literally everyone in entertainment, not only up North, but throughout the country. Then one day, while Ken and Jo were away on holiday in Italy that summer, he had an idea of forming a company with them to manage and present specific shows, distinct from his radio and television work. He felt so thrilled about it that he picked up the phone and put through a personal call to them on the shores of Lake Maggiore.

Ken and Jo, always game for anything fresh, said at once, "We're on if you say so. What shall we call it?"

Scott-Comber said that they would all think of something, and so it was settled there and then.

On their return, the three of them went into it in detail. Bill had the expertise. Jo possessed dress sense and a flair for the theatre generally. Ken would soon be qualified legally to act on that side. Nothing could be better, it seemed. All that remained at that stage was to think of a good name for the company.

"Well, we met through Sandra," Bill said, "how about Sandra Productions?"

"Perfect," they agreed. And on Christmas Eve, 1958, the company was formally registered. Basically, the plan was to act only as a management, not as theatrical agents, and they would insist on quality in order to gain a reliable reputation. One of the earliest shows they arranged was cabaret at the Royal Restaurant, Liverpool, followed by a successful show at Skegness the following summer. They decided early on to avoid big names and big fees and concentrate on entertainment. Instead of one artiste at £250, who could be a hit or a miss, they aimed for four or five virile, entertaining acts. And there was always the chance of discovering a star.

They worked from home at Oxford, with Jo doing most of the routine organization by phone and letter, and Ken and Jo went up to Manchester many week-ends. Then, while Ken was finishing his law course, Jo followed Bill around learning the ropes: entrances, exits, lighting, changes, and all the hundred and one things to be remembered about the theatre. He let her do the running order of one show, and as a result one artiste did not have enough time to make a change. But she was quick to learn from small mistakes like these. Ken and Jo both loved the atmosphere of show business, and learnt, too, not to let personal prejudice against an act necessarily influence them.

Ken especially liked the jazz side of the company, and presented one-night stands such as Humphrey Lyttelton, Nat Gonella, Mick Mulligan, and others. When Bill was editing a B.B.C. tape-recorded radio programme one day, he took Ken along to listen to it, and one of the first things Ken did was to tie up the engineers completely with a technical point to which they had no answer at all.

The routine running of the company was carried on between Manchester, Oxford, London, and other places, and to be in current touch Bill phoned Ken and Jo every night of the week without fail.

"Any news?"

"Yes, they want £150 for that act," Jo would tell him.

"Don't pay it. It's not worth more than £120."

Bill was also a very good friend indeed, and at least part of his reason for ringing regularly was to find out how Ken was keeping and contact him by the best possible way – telephone. Both Bill and Ken gained a lot and learned a lot by this attachment, Bill no less than Ken. For, in Ken, he found another outlet for his inherent talent to leave life brighter than he finds it. Bill appreciated, too, the attraction of show business for Ken and Jo, who both had to acclimatize themselves to living under their own individual clouds.

Only strength of mind such as Ken's could overcome his blindness. Yet, strangely, it is this very strength that also made it more difficult sometimes, for if he had been more servile or resigned, he might not struggled so much. But resignation to him was only another word for defeat.

Bill knew an Irish boxer once who was blinded and then affected by fits of depression so violent that he hit his head against the nearest wall in protest against it. Ken felt just as strongly as this and could become moody occasionally. He might have made a 'bitchy' remark, but, in an instant, he recovered himself and apologized. This is the extreme extent of his success.

And he got on with life, his French lessons, his talking books, and the guitar. He had a proper course of lessons on tape for the guitar, and could soon render quite reasonably *The Foggy, Foggy Dew*. But it had to be entirely by ear, of course. Ken felt the braille music, played a few notes, memorized them, and then passed on a bit farther. Playing the guitar is a two-handed job, and so there was no way for Ken of avoiding the laborious job of reading the braille and then getting his hand back on to the right stoppings again before continuing with the next phrase. Still, it was a challenge that he accepted. Sandra Productions flourished, too.

Then in the summer of 1960 came the climax of Ken's life. Bill Scott-Comber was asked if he knew any suitable subjects for the B.B.C. television feature series *It Happened to Me*. Each of these thirty-minute programmes dealt with one particular person or subject, usually of sociological interest, and created dramatic documentary impact. Bill at once thought of Ken. The idea was put forward, received official approval, and in September a B.B.C. film unit shot some amazing sequences that revealed exactly what a blind man can do – if he makes up his mind.

While Ken and Jo were staying at Lake Maggiore in 1958, they had met an English girl and an Italian motor-boat instructor, who also specialized in water-skiing. These two gave Ken some tips on skiing, and he persuaded them to let him have a go at it. On the calm waters of this lake, which is partly in Italy, partly in Switzerland, Ken tried it several times and managed to stay on the surface for several seconds.

The first of the shots the B.B.C. wanted, therefore, was one of Ken repeating his attempt at water-skiing. There was no trouble for Ken in swimming, which he did regularly. In a pool he made for the steps, or the side of the pool where he could hear voices. And in a lake or the sea, he managed just as well, except on a rocky shore, which he always avoided.

In the summer of 1957, for instance, while he and Jo were on holiday at Majorca, Ken enjoyed some superb swimming from the flat sandy beach. He liked this especially since he could be left alone safely on a beach of this sort, and did not have to be looked after all the time. He wandered up and down the beach, went in for a swim, came out and sunbathed, and strolled along the private shore till he came in touch with one or two of the others from the same hotel and had a chat with them. But the most precious thing about it all was being able to be on his own and use his own initiative for once. The lack of independence is what he really missed most, coupled with the inability to have any secrets, however small, from anyone.

Yet he had independence and enterprise enough to travel abroad twice quite alone, only meeting friends at his destinations. Once he went to Paris, the other time to Switzerland. This latter trip involved *flying* from London to Zurich, taking the *train* to Lucerne, and then a *steamer* to Weggis.

The most convenient water surface for the skiing was at South Cerney, near Cirencester. The lake bore the unpromising name of Hills Gravel Pit, but turned out to be quite a pleasant stretch of water in the heart of the West Country. Cranes were digging out gravel in the distance, while red lorries carted it off. But the mile-or-so-long lake looked inviting on an afternoon of slowly scudding clouds. Little tufts of islands grew out of the lake, and away on the far side rose a couple of dozen sticks of masts belonging to yachts drawn up ashore.

Later in the day, one or two sails streamed out across the water as local yachtsmen took to it after work. From the gravel sides of the lake, the water sloped down quite sharply to some thirty feet deep in the middle.

Jo watched the scene rather anxiously as Ken changed into his blue trunks in the little corrugated hut. When he had had time, she went in and helped him towards the man-made stretch of 'beach' before discussing the final details of his attempt with the producer and cameraman.

A fine fibreglass turbocraft, gleaming white in the sunshine, lay drawn up on the gravel, and its driver, Jean Brotherton, revved up the motor while she waited. They told her at what speed to drive out from the bank, and then tied Ken's twenty-yard line to the stern of the boat. Meanwhile Ken was shivering slightly in the breeze as he prepared to paddle into the water. He felt for the edge, and put the pair of blue skis down. Then he wriggled each foot around till he located the position for it on the ski.

With both feet securely in these rubber grips, he stood up again, swaying a little, and gripped the wooden handle attached to the line. Finally, he waded slowly into the deeper water, crouched down till it was up to his neck, and leaned back to give himself as much pressure as possible to counteract the strong pull of the boat as it suddenly started.

"Ready, Ken?"

"Okay."

Jean Brotherton looked round and the boat began to move. The line tautened, quivered, and Ken hung on to the handle. The pull hit him too sharply – and he fell forward into the water on his face. No harm was done, and the skis floated free to the surface. "Sorry about that," he called. "Don't worry. Will you have another shot?"

Ken was already fitting his feet into the skis at the water's edge, and in a couple of minutes he was ready for the next attempt. The boat lunged forward, the line snapped tight, and again Ken fell forward into the water.

"I'll have one more try," he insisted. The same routine, but this time he tried to make sure he would be ready for the shock when it came. And as the boat increased speed, he forced himself back to take the strain, so that his left leg and then the right skimmed up through the foam – and for a second, he was waterborne. And for a second, too, as he stumbled out of the water, he looked a very lone figure.

After he was dressed, Ken asked, "If this boat's as exciting as you're all saying, why can't I try to drive it?"

There were seats for three in the front and two at the stern of the turbocraft. He swung his leg over the rail of the sleek white craft, and was shown into the driving-seat behind the left-hand wheel. The demonstrator sat in the centre.

The foot controls of the turbocraft could not have been simpler and it would stop dead in exactly eight feet. The craft had a broad flat bottom that drew only three inches of water when in motion, yet somehow kept it stable at the same time. One of the distinguished drivers of this 14½-foot boat has been Donald Campbell.

When Ken heard this, he commented, "Well, if he can drive it so can I."

With a roar from the rear and a rush of air, the craft was soon shooting smoothly forward across the lake. Electrifying exhaust noise added to the excitement as Jean told Ken which way to turn the wheel.

Spray spurted out on each bow, and mixed with the mist from the turbo at the stern. Waves washed into the shore as it gathered speed. White spray, turquoise water, the breeze blowing, Ken steering. Twenty knots now, twenty-five, thirty.

"Swing round to the right," Jean shouted above the noise.

The turbocraft turned a sharp U-bend, leaving a semicircle of spray-flecks frothing into the distance. But though the turn was sharp, those on board felt comfortable all the time. Soon they were roaring around an island and rushing on towards the other end of the lake, reaching 3,800 revs. A slight shudder as they skimmed over the water, but it was only buffeting by the wind. Two complete circuits, and Ken reluctantly drove it inshore at the end of an exhilarating experience.

Then after a night in the bygone grace of Cheltenham, they set off next day down the side of the Severn Valley to Filton for Ken's final and sternest test: to drive a sports car down the Bristol Aircraft's runway. Ken had been crazy about cars ever since the early thirties, and when he was a front-seat passenger he still leant forward instinctively to feel that the choke was in.

The car he chose was an MGA, and Ken and Jo had stopped at the MG works in Abingdon on their way down to give Ken a chance to get used to the gearbox by trying it out on the special 'comparator' there. Jo drove the four wheels on to rollers and then Ken took over. As he accelerated the engine, the wheels drove the rollers, through a belt, to a fan. This emitted the terrific noise of a propeller whirring, while the wheels went on turning faster and registered the miles per hour at which the car would be travelling. A spell on this enabled Ken to get accustomed to the low gear lever with its reverse in the left position, first and second in the middle, and third and top at the right.

Jo described the colours of the car to him on their way down to Filton. He already knew its technical details: 1600 c.c., twin carburettors, and so on. It had wire wheels instead of the solid pressings more usual nowadays, and the top speed was a solid 100 m.p.h., with no cross-wind flicker. Its pinky-beige tone gave it a sleek, smart effect, and the upholstery was toned in rich red leather.

Amber landing-lights flanked the Filton runway, with its 7,275-foot length and 300-foot width. Over on the north side, a row of poplars bent back from the south-west, a sign of which way the prevailing wind blew. And to confirm it, grey clouds careered in from the Severn Estuary. A goods train tugged at a long line of trucks to the south of the airstrip, and alongside the track towered the twin hangars, with their pink curved roofs, used as the Britannia assembly halls. On the runway itself, a Bristol Britannia of Ghana Airways stood perfectly poised. Along the northern side stretched a dark outline of trees, while the concrete sections of runway rose and then dipped quite steeply out of sight to the west. And dominating the scene the whole time, the rows and banks of amber landing-lights.

The weather was bad. Ken felt the rain on his face. It gave way to a blustering cross-wind, and then returned later in the morning. It was no good yet for photography, so Ken and Jo decided to try out the runway.

Ken pulled his brown duffle-coat over his blue sweater and took his beret out of the pocket. Jo too needed headgear. She was wearing slacks, and a red, yellow, purple, and turquoise top. They put the hood up quickly and clambered into the low-slung MGA.

The plan was simple. Jo directed him to the centre of the 300-foot-wide runway at its eastern end. Once there, they flashed their headlights till the Decca radar scanner in the control tower opposite gave them a green light, indicating that all was safe to proceed. The same thing was arranged at the other end for the return run.

Ken knew the gears well by now, and the pedals seemed straightforward, so the main difficulty appeared to be the basic one of steering. He intended to get on to the course Jo called out, and to try and keep it by feeling that the spokes on the steering-wheel were in the same position. He did not grip the wheel unduly tightly and found no trouble with the mechanics generally, except that "I don't know where the hell I am."

So, they started that unique test of a blind man driving a car entirely unaided, except for directions. From the very first run, it was clear that unless someone already knew that Ken was at the wheel they could not possibly tell that the car was not being driven by a sighted person. Jo called out the directions. Ken did the rest.

The best way to convey the effect is to hear Jo: "Got the green light now. Start swinging left, Ken. Right round left. Centre of runway now. You'll have to get straight. Left a bit. Good. Righto. Straight ahead. Going straight. That's fine. Left a bit – left. Lovely. Here's the yellow line. Bring her right slightly, very slightly. We're past the hangars now. That's where we get the winds. Left a little more. Just reached 80. Start slowing down. Still keep her left. Change down now. Start to swing round right, still more . . .

"Wait for the green light. Stop her there now. Back to the centre. Line her up. Ready for the return run now. Left, left, now stop. Let her roll. Accelerate –now. Keep the wheel moving slightly, Ken. Gone over 80 then, about 88. Left. Straight. Change her down . . ."

They had done their first two-way run. The next one was coming up – with the weather still bad.

"Permission to go. Roll forward, right round at an angle. Get her straight. Not in centre of runway yet. Not quite straight yet. Righto. Let her go. Rev up. Beautifully straight. Gosh. Lot of water on the track. Going up to 60. Left, left. Bang down the centre. Revs 4,500. Rain on windscreen. Slow down, gently. Very slippery here. Left. Got to swing round. Slowly. Too fast. Slowly. Right, stop there."

"Away we go," Ken called, as Jo gave him the all-clear, and in a minute, they had travelled the return mile to the starting-line again.

Jo cut up Ken's lunch as they looked out at the clouds, still low over the field. Ken turned and said to those present, "The wind's pulling the car quite a lot. I wouldn't like to be doing it with anyone except Jo – but it's still great fun. The only other snag is that with the rain beating on the hood I get rather an enclosed feeling." Then he explained how he was getting the impression of changing speed by the stronger wind noise and slight increase in bumping over the sections of runway.

Then they walked into the open again under a speckled sky, the deep silver sunlight drying the runway. It was time to put the hood down. The first two runs were to film Ken and Jo from a car alongside. The latter car started first, as it was slower than the sports, and cruised along at 60 to 70 m.p.h. Then Ken came up from the left rear. He kept a dead steady course only ten yards away, and drew level for the filming. The two cars were travelling at 70 m.p.h. in perfect formation, before Jo acknowledged the camera car's signal and Ken shot ahead to 90 m.p.h., leaving the other trailing sadly.

A couple of runs were then wanted with the camera fitted to the bonnet of the MGA and pointing back at Ken and Jo. And finally, there were two more with the camera fixed at the rear and looking ahead over their shoulder. As the little MGA, with its registration number SRX 149, turned to make these final runs, Ken began to feel fully at ease behind the wheel, but his ambition was not yet fulfilled. Jo did not need to give him so many directions now as he edged forward towards the start.

"Wait for the green light. There it is. Right, right. Get central on runway. We can go now. Hold her steady. Speed 50. That's right. Tracking dead centre. Seventy now. Left a little. 70, 72, 75, 80 miles an hour. Left. Rev. counter 4500. 85 now, coming up to 90. 90, 92, 95.

Left a little. Slow her down. Change gear, 60 now. Left still further. Turn left more. Stop."

And so, to the final recorded run, with the tape-recorder on Jo's lap.

"You can let her go *now*. Yes, hold that. Speed 50. Rev. counter 4500, and rising. Crossing the yellow line. Dead central. No, left a little. Left still. 80 miles an hour. You're doing 85. 90 now. Rev. counter 5000. 95 coming up any second. 100 wavering on the speedo. 100 – jolly good. Slow down a bit. Steady. That's fine . . ."

A hundred miles an hour. An ambition achieved. There would be many more ahead, but back in the control-room Ken Revis relaxed into an armchair, took out his matches, struck one slowly, and felt for the bowl of his pipe.

Shall I ever see again? Ken knew the answer to that a long time ago. But he still says, "If only . . ." Then he pushed what he missed most under the surface, so that no one would know, and grinned and bore it.

He could never be really reconciled. There were always so many things bound to irritate and frustrate him. Since he was determined not to lead a neutral life, he found himself up for most of the time, and down occasionally. Jo, too, was active and animated usually, only moody once in a while.

"If only . . ." It was the little things Ken had to overcome. The bigger fact he had learned to live with, to accept. The car runs out of petrol and he is helpless. Or they reach Manchester at 10 p.m. with Jo too tired to drive farther. If only he could have seen, Ken would have told her to wrap up in a rug and sit back while he drove her home to Oxford.

Although he loved to get out and about, home was best for Ken: it was where he felt his loss least. The door, the fire, the switches, the television set, the whole familiarity was friendly. Yet he had to be careful not to stay in too much.

He felt worst when in crowded places with strangers who could only be a blur of voices. And he sensed quickly when people find him a trouble. People might have failed to communicate with him through either embarrassment or pure thoughtlessness. Not intentionally, but just by their inability to project themselves into his position, to imagine how he felt and what he needed. Simple lack of imagination.

The little things mattered. The phone, for instance, which meant so much. Ken could not see, so he had to make the most of what was left. His life, as a result, was inevitably a struggle, but an amazingly successful one.

His sense of humour helped him in the daily encounter which was his life. He tried not to let situations knock it out of him. His success can be judged by his jokes about being blind. Like the one to a colleague who had a new pair of glasses. Ken tried them on and said, "Well, I don't think they're much good – I can't see a single thing through them!"

And he loved to tell horrified listeners how he cleaned his eyes with that famous metal-polish! These lighter asides hid a courage which was deep, for the very reason that it was so completely concealed.

One of Ken's problems had always been keeping up to date with things. He liked to know the news in the paper, and he 'watched' television regularly – including such programmes as *Panorama* and *Tonight*. His job, too, helpd him by making him keep abreast of the times. As assistant to the public relations officer of the Nuffield Organization, he wrote Press releases and articles; met people from newspapers, magazines, film and TV companies; and looked after the cars kept for road testing by journalists.

Ken had never seen a safety-belt, so he once had a run in a car fitted with one, sitting in the passenger seat and undergoing crash-stops at 45 m.p.h. Cars seemed to be integral to his life and, in fact, offset his lack of personal mobility, which was one of the worst losses he endured. One of his last forms of transport was a glider, which he learnt to fly.

Ambitions are far harder to achieve for those who never had, or have lost, their sight, who must take the type of job they can do. Yet Ken had to admit that he achieved much more than he had thought possible on that first far-off day he went to St Dunstan's.

How had life changed from what it might have been? He had a love of bridge-building – especially over water – and he would have achieved this ambition if he had not been blinded. Probably he and Jo would have gone abroad for the first ten years after the war. But he did not dwell on what might have been; he accepted that much. He would never build bridges, or dam great waterways.

Not surprisingly, Ken found it hard to "look ahead," yet he always remained ready to try something new. To him, fresh experiences represented the renewal of life. The blinding flash may have maimed him, but his spirited survived.